MILLER'S BOLT

D1512099

MILLER'S BOLT

A Modern Business Parable

THOMAS STIRR

Foreword by Ken Blanchard

Addison-Wesley Publishing Company, Inc.

Reading, Massachusetts Menlo Park, California New York
Don Mills, Ontario Harlow, England Amsterdam Bonn
Sydney Singapore Tokyo Madrid San Juan Paris Seoul
Milan Mexico City Taipei

Information on behavioral dimensions is based on the Personal Profile System®, © Copyright 1994, Carlson Learning Company. All rights reserved.

Personal Profile System® is a registered trademark of Carlson Learning Company. DiSC™ is a trademark of Carlson Learning Company.

For additional information on the Personal Profile System, DiSC Dimensions of Behavior, and Carlson Learning Company, please call our Fax-on- Demand telephone number, 1-800-777-9897.

Library of Congress Cataloging-in-Publication Data

Stirr, Thomas.
    Miller's bolt : a modern business parable / Thomas Stirr :
foreword by Ken Blanchard.
        p. cm.
    Includes index.
    ISBN 0-201-14379-8
    I. Title.
PS3569.T546M55 1997
813.54—dc21   96-40935
                                                      CIP

Addison-Wesley books are available at special discounts for bulk purchases by corporations, institutions, and other organizations. For more information, please contact the Corporate, Government, and Special Sales Department, Addison-Wesley Publishing Company, Reading, MA 01867, 1-800-238-9682.

Jacket design by Jean Seal
Text design and composition by Carol Woolverton Studio

1 2 3 4 5 6 7 8 9-DOH-0100999897
First printing, April 1997

For my wife, Rosemary,
and our three children,
Adam, Eric and Erin,
who prove that life truly is a festival!

There is nothing either good or bad,
but thinking makes it so.
—*William Shakespeare*

Foreword

IN A TOUGH, COMPETITIVE WORLD THERE IS ONE NAGGING thought that keeps gnawing at each of us: "How do I improve my performance."

If there was ever a parable written for today, it is *Miller's Bolt*. This masterful story draws you through its pages with realistic characters and situations and delivers a powerhouse of ideas. Quite simply, *Miller's Bolt* is a must read if you genuinely want to improve yourself and the quality of your life. It is more than just another "how-to" manual—it is a creative journey that anyone who hopes to be successful must take.

There are many personal management books on the market today, but few deliver the goods as effectively as *Miller's Bolt*. No dry lectures here. As Thomas weaves this parable, you live the techniques with the characters. You experience their pain and frustration and the modern stresses they feel.

As the story unfolds, Thomas guides you through the performance spiral. It is a simple and logical process that combines time-tested personal management principles with easy-to-use project management skills. *Miller's Bolt* reminds us that our performance is never static. We are either getting a little bit better, or a little bit worse every day. It confirms that we cannot conveniently divide our lives into home and work segments. Each part of our life profoundly affects the other. And finally, *Miller's Bolt* puts the onus for our performance squarely where it belongs, with each one of us.

So sit back and enjoy the story that Thomas Stirr has crafted for us. *Miller's Bolt* offers you a treasure chest of powerful tools to help you improve your performance right now. Choosing to use them could be the difference between your success or personal obsolescence.

Ken Blanchard
coauthor
The One-Minute Manager® and
Everyone's a Coach

Acknowledgments

Thanks to

Sharon Broll, of Addison Wesley Longman, for her deft editorial hand and suggestions.

Bob Diforio, of D4EO Unltd. Literary Agency, for taking a gamble on an unknown author.

Merrilee Cole and **Dr. Linda Rening**, of Carlson Learning Company, for their assistance with copyright permissions.

Brian Connelly, of Blanchard Training and Development, for opening a door, then becoming a friend.

Michele Waters, Allan Waters, Wendy Tryhorn, and **Vanessa Parker**, for their suggestions during the early stages of *Miller's Bolt*.

Larry Hughes, Susan Cox, and **Barry Siskind** for their help along the road named Serendipity.

John Vickruck, for being a legal eagle extraordinaire and a friend.

Ginette Doucette, for continually improving her corner of the universe.

Ted Light, for his ongoing input and his ability to separate church and state.

Very Special Thanks to

Ken Blanchard, for his years of encouragement and for providing the foreword for this book.

Peter Comrie, a friend like no other, for helping to keep the light shining and the path in sight.

1

KAREN WOKE BEFORE THE ALARM. SHE MOVED THE CLOCK setting to the off position just in time to save herself from a barrage of shrill beeps. Judging from the noise in the kitchen, Jim hadn't left for work yet. She threw on her robe as she went down the hall to greet him.

"Good mornin', hon," she patted him playfully on the rump.

"Mornin'."

"I thought you'd have left for work by now, you're usually gone by seven."

"Yeah, I know. Felt a little tired this morning. Thought I could use a few extra winks."

Karen reached for a cup to pour some coffee from the pot Jim always made in the morning.

"No point burning yourself out. You've been putting in a lot of extra time. Anyway, it's nice to see you this early in the day," she said.

Despite her light tone Karen's lips were drawn tight. She looked at Jim pensively. He'd been off his schedule for a while.

"How are things at work?" she asked.

"You know . . . the same old thing. It's alright. What about you?"

"It's always busy at the end of the month," Karen replied. "I'll never understand why house buyers always want to close on the thirtieth. They must think their lawyers can simply clone themselves and do fifteen things at once."

"I know the feeling."

"You OK, Jim? You've had a few days like this lately. It's not like you, especially for this long."

"I don't know. Maybe I'm just getting tired of all the B.S. and political stuff going on. Seems almost impossible to get anyone to agree on anything without going through hell. I'll be fine. Just need to get a bit more rest, maybe exercise a bit to refuel the old jets."

"Remember, Jennifer has figure skating tonight. She'd be thrilled if you could make it. I think she may get a badge and go into the next level."

"Six-fifteen?"

"Uh huh."

"Do my best to be there. See you tonight."

He gave her a kiss and a hug. "Thanks for caring about me, Karen. Don't worry, I'll be fine."

"I know. Never been anything we couldn't beat before."

Jim grabbed his briefcase and headed for the car. He gave Karen a wave as he pulled away from the driveway. She waved back. He didn't know what he'd done to be so lucky.

There was one saving grace about sleeping in: traffic would be pretty light at this hour. He'd arrive a little late, maybe eight-forty-five. No big deal.

Jim pulled into the office parking lot at eight-forty. "Not bad!" he thought. "At least I'll have some time to get organized for the meeting." He walked in and nodded hello to the receptionist.

"Good morning, Mr. Manion. Mr. Bowerman has been waiting for you for almost forty-five minutes. He's getting a coffee right now."

Jim had forgotten to check his schedule yesterday before leaving the office and had overlooked the early-morning meeting. The guilt pangs were immediate.

Bowerman appeared from around the corner.

"Sorry about keeping you waiting," Jim said, extending his hand. "Had a bit of a personal crisis this morning. Come straight in, and we can get right to the issues you wanted to discuss."

Bowerman went through the paces of his lengthy sales pitch, showing Jim the latest issue of the magazine and carefully guiding him through the details of the current audit statement. He then used some client testimonial letters to set up the close.

"As you can see, Mr. Manion, our magazine has the right audience, our circulation is tightly audited, and we're generating good leads for our other advertisers. I'm sure we can deliver the same value for you. Can we help you move some product by including your advertising in twelve issues next year?"

Jim felt even more guilty. The magazine wasn't really a primary target for his company's advertising, but he felt compelled to hold out some hope for Bowerman.

"Give me a few more weeks to finalize our budget. Follow up the first of next month, we should know our final numbers by then. You've presented a good case today. We'll see what we can do to fit your book in."

Bowerman confirmed a follow-up date, entered it in his tickler file, thanked Jim for the appointment, and found his own way out.

As Bowerman left, Jim's mind was racing, "Jeez . . . it's already nine-forty! I wish I'd never made that appointment. It would have been much easier to just brush it off. Now I've got that damn management committee meeting in twenty minutes and haven't even got time to prepare."

Jim had been agonizing over the meeting all week. He just couldn't seem to see eye to eye with a lot of the other members of the management committee. Lynne Donato, the vice president of manufacturing, always seemed to take a position contrary to his regardless of the logic he presented. A couple of serious battles had erupted between them during the past year.

The national sales manager, Ted Wilkinson, was no better. He had that swagger that comes from going to the "right" school. The "right" degree. The "right" connections. Jim felt like he was under the microscope whenever he was in Ted's presence. Jim was growing tired of Ted's callous put-downs of other people, his snide way of referring to other schools as "Basketweave U."

Many of the other committee members were individual burrs under Jim's saddle. All the meetings seemed to end up the same lately with everyone bickering and staking out political ground. Little if anything was getting accomplished.

"At least I've got twenty minutes to gather my background briefs and budgets," thought Manion.

Katherine Fisher was in her office gathering papers as well. She had been president for the past seven years and took pride in the management team she'd built. But there was an uneasiness about her today that had been building for some time.

Katherine had a reputation as a tough but fair leader. She believed the best way to keep a company profitable was to hire good people and give them a lot of rein. Over the years she had seldom had to yank any of them back in.

She was concerned. The numbers hadn't looked as good as they should have the last couple of quarters, and some of the cohesiveness seemed to have disappeared from the management team. She put a half dozen key documents in a file and left for the meeting. "Well, girl, today's the day to get the ship back on course."

Katherine greeted her key managers then got straight to the point. "Let's go over next year's plan again. We've got to get our budgets in line for the board meeting presentation in two weeks. We haven't made as much progress as I would have liked the past couple of meetings, but today is D-Day. We're not leaving until another 1.5 is trimmed from the operating budget."

"Yeah, yeah, yeah," Jim thought. "It's the same old bunk every meeting. When are we going to whip these prima donnas into shape? We'll just sit here for hours and argue about trivial issues."

"OK, folks, let's go around the table and review your current budgets and get some cost-cutting ideas on the table." Fisher made notes as each member of the management committee took turns presenting a brief overview. All eyes were soon focused on Manion.

"Your turn, Jim. What have you got?" asked Fisher.

Manion's eyes darted around the table, then at the file folder in front of him. "I think I've got a problem with this process. How can we sit here as a management group and slash budgets knowing full well that we're expected to increase sales and profits next year? I don't see how we can logically expect that to happen, especially if we hack our marketing programs to bits."

"Hey, if anyone's ass is on the line, it's mine," quipped Wilkinson. "If the sales department can cut expenses, so can marketing."

"Well, maybe it's a little easier for the sales department to find some fat," Manion countered. "All you have to do is cancel a few lunches and play a few less rounds of golf."

"People, let's get back on track." Fisher's gaze fell on

Manion. "Jim, this isn't a voluntary exercise. We need to cut expenses, and from what I've heard so far this morning, we've still got a long way to go. What can you offer up?"

"Katherine, you know better than anyone in this room that I can justify the costs of every program that's on the marketing plan in terms of generating a positive ROI. We've got the best tracking system in the industry, hell maybe even in the entire country."

"No one is questioning that, Jim."

"Then how can we justify slashing programs that are absolutely essential to the company's growth?"

"Finding ways to increase sales and profits is something we'll need to deal with later. The political reality is that unless we go into the board meeting with a reduced operating budget, we'll get crucified."

"You mean we can't fight for programs that we know are working? What the hell do I have to do to convince people here that money spent on marketing isn't an expense?" Manion grabbed a handful of reports from his file folder and slammed them down on the table. "Marketing has got more analysis than any other department in this company to prove that every dollar we're spending is generating profits for the company. We've probably got more proof than all of you put together."

Fisher's eyes burned into Manion. "Jim, everyone at this table agrees that marketing has done a superb job tracking the ROI on programs. That doesn't change the purpose of this meeting."

Manion's eyes locked with Fisher's then fell back to the file folder in front of him as he nodded his agreement.

It was almost noon when the meeting adjourned. Somehow they had found the 1.5. A good chunk from Jim's budget. He was tight jawed when he left the room.

"Jim, do you have any plans for lunch?"

"No, Katherine, I'm open today. What's up?"

"Let's go grab a bite. I need to talk to you a bit."

They exchanged small talk in the car on the way to the restaurant. Jim thought that the luncheon was the president's way of trying to make peace after gouging his budget, but he suddenly felt a little uneasy when Katherine asked for a table in the back corner of the restaurant.

"Jim, I want to talk to you about how things have been going lately. I've got some concerns about how the team is functioning. We've got a small management group, and it's important that we maintain a good working environment."

"Katherine, I couldn't agree more," Jim responded. "I've also had difficulty with how things have been progressing the past couple of months."

"I'm glad to hear that. You've made a lot of significant contributions over the years, and I really value your input. If things are going to get better, we need to have you on our side."

"I think we really need to take a good look at how the responsibilities are structured. Some of the folks like Ted just don't look at the whole picture when . . . "

Katherine gently interrupted Jim.

"Let's not talk about the others." Her eyes were in sharp focus, her hands gently clasped on the table. "Jim, you've been here for over four years. We have always been able to count on you to bring a fresh perspective to the table. Lately, I don't know."

"What do you mean, I don't know?" Jim leaned forward, feeling his face flush. "Katherine, you know what I've done for the company over the years. I've busted my butt getting things done. I redesigned our control programs and developed an ROI tracking capability second to none. Just think about all the programs I've introduced. We'd have never gotten this far without my ideas and effort."

Katherine remained calm. "I realize that, Jim. That's why we're having this discussion. You have been a very valuable member of the team and have made significant contributions. But things change. You've changed."

Jim respected Katherine. She'd made it the hard way, coming up through the ranks. No one questioned her intellect, drive, or abilities. She'd hired him and spent time helping him develop. She listened to his ideas, had even stuck her neck out to champion some of his more radical plans.

That didn't stop Jim's heart from racing or his throat from getting dry, and the sudden churning in his stomach. He struggled against the strange mixture of disbelief and anger that threatened to overwhelm him.

"Katherine, I've always valued our relationship. You've got to help me with this one. I just don't get it."

"Jim, your attitude's changed. Your perspective. It's like you come to work looking for a brawl. Your view's a lot more narrow. Aggressive. You can't be effective unless you bring an open mind to the party. That's always been your big strength. Something this company needs."

"Come on, you know we've got some real pigheaded people on the management committee. They're only interested in building their little kingdoms. If I didn't get more focused and aggressive they'd run right over me."

"Jim, you've worked with most of these people for at least three years. Think back . . . do you ever remember the group being as fractured as it is today? From my perspective, they really haven't changed. The way you relate to them sure has. Look at what happened in the management meeting this morning when you behaved so defensively about budgets. There was no need to jump down Ted's throat the way you did."

"I can't believe you're siding with . . . "

"It's not taking sides. I'm trying to get you in touch with reality. Things can't continue the way they are now. We need to get a grip on this situation before it gets beyond the point where we can fix it."

2

Lunch had taken longer than Katherine Fisher had anticipated. The drive back from the restaurant was quiet, but she couldn't help noticing the muscles twitching at the corner of Jim's jaw.

As soon as she was back in her office, Katherine called Philippe Fontaine, the vice president of human resources. "Philippe, I was wondering if you might have time this afternoon to pull Jim Manion's personnel file and go over it with me."

"Can you give me about a half hour? I just need to finish up a brief meeting."

"Fine. Let's make it my office at two-forty-five."

Philippe quickly finished off the business at hand and retrieved Manion's file. It was unusual for Katherine to request this type of meeting. He did a quick inventory of the file to make sure that all the necessary documents were in place. Then he briefly reviewed the performance appraisals to get a sense of what the meeting might be about.

"Come in, Philippe, and please close the door behind you. I have some concerns and need your advice." Katherine's greeting was more direct than usual.

"Perhaps you could give me an overview of your con-

cerns. I've brought Manion's file with me," Philippe replied as
he sat down at the small conference table in Katherine's office.

"Jim's been a very good performer since he joined us,"
said Fisher, "but things haven't been going well the past six
to nine months. Lately it's much worse. He's become very
abrasive with the other senior managers."

"Katherine, there's nothing in his file that even hints at
any performance deficiencies. He's due for a review in about
three months. The most current documents on file show
that he is one of our top producers."

"That's the strange thing, Philippe. In terms of the specific tasks he performs, he still is. I just don't know whether
we can afford to keep him."

"We'd be treading on very thin ice to let him go without
cause and a documented case. If he pressed the issue and
went to court, the judgment could be substantial."

"I realize that. If we need to do something, we'll make
sure that the settlement is more than fair. What do you
think it would cost us?"

"Do you want to be absolutely safe?"

Katherine nodded.

"Well, with four years' tenure and very solid performance reviews, we'd need to go at least six months. Since
we chased Jim through a headhunter and took him away
from a long-standing relationship with his previous em-
ployer, we'd probably need to go to twelve, maybe fifteen
months. With outplacement counseling and benefits extension, we're looking at a very expensive package. Now that's
being absolutely safe. If he went to any labor lawyer in the
country they'd tell him to take the money and run."

Katherine looked at Philippe for a few moments without
speaking then turned her gaze toward the window. "God . . .
sometimes things just aren't easy. You know, I hired Jim.
He's been the driving force behind some of the best things
we've done over the last four years. Remember that revolu-
tionary segmentation strategy he came up with?"

Philippe countered, "Katherine, it's out of character for you to make a snap decision. Especially one like this. There's lots of other things we can do before we have to look at something as drastic as termination. Let's discuss some other options."

"You're right. But then, you always are." The tightness in Katherine's face had eased somewhat. "I want to put all of my concerns on the table for you to review. Then I'd like to discuss any ideas you have."

She walked over to her desk and picked up the telephone. "Amy, this is Katherine Fisher. Please hold all my calls as well as Philippe Fontaine's for the balance of the afternoon. Is Ted in today? Good. If anything appears urgent from an operations standpoint, put it through to him. Thanks." She dialed another four digits. "Hello Ted, . . . Katherine. I'm going to be tied up for a few hours. I've asked Amy to put my urgent calls through to you to stickhandle. Thanks."

By four-fifteen Philippe and Katherine had reviewed Jim Manion's situation thoroughly and had come to an agreement on a plan of action.

"OK. I'll speak to him early next week and lay out our suggestions for improvement as well as a timetable. I'll document the meeting."

"Philippe, do you really think we need to build a file on this?"

"It would definitely help if we got into court."

"We talked about giving this situation three months to turn around. I doubt whether we could build a sufficient file to be of much help if there was litigation anyway," said Katherine.

"Well, that's true. But there is a company policy. . . . "

"Philippe, I know Jim pretty well. I think documenting would only get his hackles raised further. If there's going to be any hope of turning this situation around, we'll need Jim to be as open-minded as possible."

"OK, Katherine, as long as you realize that without any documentation the cost of a separation package will be higher."

"In the bigger picture it won't make that much difference. We owe him the best we can do. I'd rather not blemish his reputation. Besides, to build a decent file to support a dismissal, we'd need to wait at least six months . . . probably up to a year. That would only serve to disrupt our management team even more. It will be less painful for everyone to put a good package together and let all parties get on with business."

"So our timetable is still three months?"

"Yes. If the situation hasn't improved noticeably by then, I want you to put a separation package together that will keep us out of court and allow Jim sufficient time and support to get placed somewhere else."

"Katherine, I hope it doesn't come to that. But, I've found that once an employee's attitude goes sour, it's really tough to get it back on track. Especially if they go into the denial stage where they blame the company for actions they're bringing on themselves."

"This is so frustrating, Philippe," said Katherine. "Especially since Jim's personal performance is still good. He just doesn't realize that it's not enough to just do his job. If he's having a negative impact on other people around him, he's a liability. We can't afford the costs of a bad attitude. Especially in management ranks."

"Well, Katherine, with a little luck and some maturity on Manion's part, we just might be able to straighten things out."

It's not enough to just do your job. If you have a negative impact on other people around you, you're a liability.

It was nearly three in the afternoon when Jim Manion arrived home from work. The house would be quiet for another hour. Jim thought about how he was going to explain being home so early. How do you tell your family that the boss told you to take the rest of the day off so you could think about whether you have a future with the company? How do you tell them you're afraid your career is headed for the toilet?

His thoughts had run the gamut during lunch, competing in an emotional decathlon. Anger. Guilt. Betrayal. Worthlessness. Disbelief and more. And at the end of it, there was Katherine's calm suggestion to "take the rest of the day off and think about where you're going."

"Where I'm going?" Manion thought. "I don't even know how I got here! From hero to bum in less than a year."

He paced around the kitchen, unsure of what to do with himself. "Well, at least I can see Jennifer skate tonight," he thought. Jim pictured his eight-year-old daughter when she had first started skating lessons three years ago: bent ankles, arms waving like a whirling dervish, hockey helmet rolling around on her head, her speed measured in feet per minute.

Manion decided to distract himself by making dinner for the family. He cracked a smile thinking about the ribbing he'd get from the kids. They'd eat, but not without holding their throats, gagging, and claiming to be poisoned. "You'd think I never cook for them, the way they carry on," he mused. Then he realized he hadn't made dinner in months. In fact, he'd been getting in so late from work he couldn't even remember the last time he'd eaten with them on a weekday. Manion decided on a chicken stir-fry. They could eat early and all go to the arena.

The counter quickly filled with the ingredients of "Manion's special stir-fry": carrots, celery, onions, green pepper, fresh ginger, and garlic, soy sauce, chicken broth mix, cayenne pepper, and finally some Tabasco and Worcestershire sauces.

To really get in the mood, Manion put on his "Born to Burn" barbecue apron and the flopped-over chef's hat Karen had given him as a joke a few years ago. He grabbed a package of chicken breasts from the freezer and popped them into the microwave to thaw. "The first step in any modern dinner is to nuke the meat," Jim thought. "The next is to make yourself believe you can actually cook."

While the chicken was in the microwave, Manion called Karen at her office. "Ms. Okira please. Hello, Ms. Okira. This is Born to Burn Catering calling. I've been instructed to request your presence at a special dinner at your residence today. Dinner will be served at five P.M. sharp. If you're late you will go hungry and be left alone to do dishes. Plus there will be no special after-dinner treats." Karen was still giggling as Jim hung up the telephone.

Dinner went well. The children gagged and joked as expected, Jim and Karen exchanged smiles throughout the meal. The four of them left at six o'clock for the skating arena.

Huddled under one of the ceiling-mounted radiant heaters, Jim, Karen, and ten-year-old Bryan watched Jennifer's spins and twirls. She really had improved. Jim felt guilty for missing so many lessons.

"What brings you home so early?" Karen asked as she turned to Jim. "Not that I'm complaining."

"Been spending too many hours at the office lately. I thought it was time for some of the more important things in life," Jim replied, forcing a smile.

"When did Jennifer learn to do that?" Jim asked, a bit taken aback as he watched her leap into the air.

"I don't know, maybe three months ago," Karen replied.

Jim felt uncomfortable. He was becoming a stranger in his own family. "I guess I haven't been around as much as I should have the past few months."

"It's been a busy time," was Karen's reply. "Besides, that was then, and this is now." She nuzzled in closer to him.

Jennifer kept looking up into the crowd to make sure her father was watching her. Jim could feel his daughter's pride every time she completed a twirl or a jump. He saw her eyes continually dart up to the stands and the smile she tried to hide.

After skating Jim suggested that the family go to the local video store and rent a movie. Karen protested that it was a school night and the children wouldn't get enough sleep. The issue was put to a rare family vote. Predictably, Karen lost.

It was almost quarter to eight when the family arrived back home. "OK, Bryan, you get the popper out and the bag of popping corn. Jennifer, get some butter out of the fridge and salt from the cupboard. It's showtime!" Jim exclaimed. They quickly got the popcorn prepared. Karen took some ice cubes from the freezer and poured the soda. They all sat on the carpet in front of the television, digging into the popcorn, slurping their drinks, and laughing at the movie.

"OK, kids, let's get those teeth brushed, glasses on the counter, PJ's on. . . . Dad'll put you to bed." Jim tickled each of the kids as they tried to dash past him.

"I'll take the movie back at lunch tomorrow. I've got a couple of hours between client meetings," offered Karen. "You know, for a kids' movie, it wasn't too bad."

"I'll try to make it home on time tomorrow," Jim replied. "I really enjoyed spending time with the kids today." He gave her a wink and chased the children upstairs to their rooms.

After the children were in bed, Jim came back downstairs and made some coffee. Cups in hand, he and Karen sat on the sofa.

"I had sort of an interesting day today," Jim began. "Actually it was a helluva day."

"Good or bad?" Karen asked.

"I'm not sure."

"That sounds somewhat ominous."

"Well . . . I guess that's a good way to describe it. We had a management committee meeting today and finally got the operating budget pared down to where it needed to be."

"That's good, isn't it?"

"Most of it was from my area."

"That never used to bother you much before."

"Yeah, I know. Anyway, it wasn't really the meeting that got to me. It was lunch. Katherine and I went out at her suggestion. Then she laid this heavy load on me that she was concerned about my ability to work with the team. Said I was getting really disruptive."

"How did you feel about that?"

"I don't know. Ticked off, I guess, at least at first. I keep on going back and forth, from thinking the whole thing was just a bad dream, to feeling mad and betrayed. If it had been anyone other than Katherine telling me, I probably would have just got mad and stayed that way."

"She's always been fair to you."

"That's what really shook me up. She's not the kind of boss to say that kind of stuff just to get you going. She must really feel that way."

"Did she give you any examples of why she's concerned?"

"Yeah, the meeting didn't go too well today. She said I was very defensive about my budget and got aggressive with the other managers. The thing that really surprised me was when she said my behavior had been out of line for quite a while."

"So you took the rest of the day off to think about it?"

"Her suggestion, and it was probably a good one. It scares you. When something like this comes out of left field at you. . . . You don't know how to react. How you're supposed to feel about it. What you're supposed to do."

"How serious is it?"

"She said we needed to get a handle on it before it got past the point of being able to fix it."

"So the patient isn't terminal?"

"No, she definitely left me with the impression that we could still work it out."

"We've been through rough spots before. We'll get past this one too."

"Karen, we've worked things out before, but not something like this. I'm not even sure I know what's really wrong. I sure as heck don't know how to fix it. When you've spent almost your whole career being a top performer, it really rocks you when your boss asks you to think about your future with the company."

"What do you think will happen next?"

"I don't know. Maybe I'll get some kind of performance letter on my personnel file. Warnings. You know, the pre-firing stuff."

"Do you think they'll have a case?"

"Not really. My section's doing well. Katherine kept talking about my ability to work with the other members of the team. Not my personal performance."

"Look. If worse comes to worse, they'll have to give you a good package. Probably a year or more. We can easily get by on that for eighteen, maybe twenty-four months. That'll be plenty of time to find something else."

"Karen, I don't want a package. I like what I do. I like the company. I have moments when things get to me, but it's good overall. I just want to fix things and get past this."

"Well, they're going to have to talk to you more about it, that's for sure. Tomorrow's Thursday. When do you think you'll find out more?"

"Not till next week. I think they'll give me a couple of days to cool down before stage two."

"What about your friend Peter? He's got a lot of good experience in this area. Maybe he'll have some ideas that could be useful. And I know somewhere you can get free legal advice."

Jim tweaked her nose. "Free advice, eh? Do you know why lawyers never get eaten by sharks?"

Karen shook her head.

"Professional courtesy."

Karen tossed a cushion at him. "Well, it's nice to see your warped sense of humor coming back!"

"They may have painted a bull's-eye on my back, but they haven't shot me yet."

"I seem to remember a promise for some after-dinner treats. Any interest?"

"A gentleman never reneges on a promise."

"I was hoping you'd say that."

3

The hot water from the shower felt good on Jim's face. He turned around and dropped his head forward, letting the water massage the back of his neck. He felt more energized this morning. He'd even beat the alarm clock. Amazing what the threat of losing your job could do.

It always helped to be able to talk to Karen. She'd listen and ask questions, but she'd seldom tell him what to do. Somehow just talking to her helped clarify things.

Jim had decided he was going to keep his nose to the grindstone and avoid confrontations at work. He needed time to sort out his emotions. He didn't want to make things worse. Above all, he wanted the chance to talk to his friend Peter Miller.

Manion had met Peter Miller at a university-sponsored management seminar almost a decade ago. They ended up in the same case study group and hit it off immediately. Peter was one of those rare souls who seemed to have an instant understanding of the most complex issues. Not only that, he could break an issue down and explain it to others in very simple, unpatronizing terms.

Jim had never met anyone quite like Peter Miller before. Miller was consumed by his interest in people, what they

19

thought, what they had to say. He was so intense he could be intimidating at first. But there was also a sincerity and a gentleness about him, and people got an immediate sense that they could trust him.

Manion's friendship with Miller had developed over time. First they had exchanged telephone numbers and would make the odd call to one another to discuss business issues, then they would meet for the occasional lunch. Within a few years they had become fast friends.

Peter Miller was an independent psychologist. At one time he had specialized in outplacement counseling; now he was in the business of helping organizations deal with change. Peter chuckled about all the buzzwords people used to try to describe his services: "empowerment counseling," "organizational reengineering," and "adaptive restructuring."

To Peter, his business was pretty simple. It was nothing more than "helping people get along, focusing on goals, and measuring progress."

It was seven-thirty when Jim Manion arrived at work. He came armed with a list of priorities he had developed the night before. By nine-fifteen, he had knocked off the first three items. He was determined to make it a good day.

About nine-thirty, Jim picked up the telephone and called Peter. "Good morning! How's my favorite independent psychologist, born in February, whose initials are P.M.?"

"Dangerous!" was Miller's reply.

"Peter, what's your schedule like the next couple of days?"

"I'm pretty well snookered until the middle of next week."

"I need to see you."

"Business or personal?"

"Personal business."

"Well then, how about after work tonight? Maybe six o'clock? I could meet you at my office or at the pub. Your choice."

"Let's make it your office. I need some quiet."

"If you need quiet, why come visit the biggest windbag you know?"

"I don't know any better, . . . and, besides, I'm a masochist with severely limited brain power."

"And not too good-looking either!"

Manion chuckled. "Peter, seriously."

"I was serious. You're not good-looking."

"Six o'clock. Your office. See you then." Manion smiled as he hung up the phone. Not everyone had a friend like Miller.

The balance of the day was uneventful. As he expected, Manion received an e-mail message from Philippe Fontaine requesting a meeting on the following Tuesday. Jim sent a quick reply to confirm. "Might as well tackle this thing head-on," he thought. "The sooner I discover whether there is a future here, the sooner I can get on with my life."

Manion kept focused throughout the day. By five he had knocked off most of the items on his priority list. He suddenly realized that he hadn't even stopped for lunch. "Man, I haven't had a day this productive in a long time," he thought. "And I still have lots of energy left. Maybe I should plan out the hot items for tomorrow so I can get rolling again in the morning."

By half past five Jim Manion had finished his priority list for the next day, cleaned his desk, answered a few late e-mail messages, and was on the way to meet with Peter Miller.

■ ■ ■

Miller's office was an exercise in organized mayhem. Files were piled everywhere: on his desk, on top of his file cabinets, spread over the coffee table, and on an oval table he used for client group meetings. One wall was completely covered with dozens of framed pictures of pets, children, and holiday adventures given to him by friends.

In marked contrast to the chaos everywhere else, on the wall directly behind Peter Miller's desk there was only one thing: a framed photograph of a stainless-steel bolt. It stood upright, balancing on its head against a background of indigo blue. In the foreground was a tangle of metal shavings and a battle-scarred wrench. The lighting in the shot was spectacular. Every subtle detail on the bolt had been captured: the cut and angle of every thread, every minute blemish in the metal.

Miller had commissioned the country's leading industrial photographer to take the shot and had bought the photographer's copyright and original transparency. He kept the film in his safety-deposit box.

Jim arrived at Miller's office just before six. He knocked twice on the office door then tried the handle. Peter had left the door open for him.

"Hey James, come on in!" Miller greeted his guest. "Take off your coat and put your feet up. Got some coffee left if you'd like some."

"Boy, that's an overly warm greeting. Are you going to charge me for this meeting?" Manion laughed as he draped his coat over one of the chairs. "Coffee sounds good. How's business doing?"

"I'd actually like the world a lot more if my business weren't doing so well. It's pretty brutal out there. Everybody's feeling squeezed."

"I can identify with that."

"A lot of companies are slashing people left and right trying to cut costs," Miller continued. "They cut people with no real vision or plan. Then productivity goes down the toilet, and the bottom line doesn't improve like they thought it would. So they cut some more."

"A vicious cycle."

"Absolutely. And when the blood's about knee-deep, management starts to wake up to the fact that what they're doing isn't working. That's when they call me, just before they've destroyed the company."

"Peter, I guess that's why I'm here. Looks like I'm probably going to be one of the targets of the cost cutting you're talking about." Jim looked at Miller and took a deep breath. "I'm not sure what I can do about it."

"Well, sport, I hate to sound callous, but if it's a straight cost-cutting issue, all you can hope for is the best package you can get. How do you know your head may be on the chopper?" asked Miller.

"Had lunch with the president yesterday. She didn't pull any punches. Told me if the situation didn't get sorted out, I'd be on my way."

"Situation? You mean financial, the company's taking a bath?"

"No. Profits are down a little, but we're still making pretty good returns. She claimed that I haven't been getting along with the other managers. The way I figure it, she's using that as an excuse to axe me."

"What kind of person is she?" Miller looked quizzical.

"I've always known her to be a straight shooter."

"Any reason why she'd change now?" Peter asked.

"Not that I can see. She really caught me off guard with her comments. It seemed so out of character."

"Out of character for her to make them, or that you were the subject?"

Jim Manion paused. "The latter I guess. You've known me for years. I've always been a top performer."

"Things can change."

"Oh thanks! I thought you were a friend!"

"I've got my business consultant hat on, Jim. No reason to get defensive with me."

"You're right, . . . sorry." Manion took a couple of sips of coffee. "I don't want to get cut. I don't want a package. I just don't know what to do."

The two men talked for over half an hour, sometimes leaning forward, intense, at others, flopping around on their chairs sharing a laugh. Jim sometimes paced the floor, and at one point Peter made paper airplanes, feigning disinterest, waiting for Jim to open up.

"I don't know, Peter. Can I help it if a person needs to be a little more aggressive than usual to get things done?"

"I see. . . . So your modus operandi has changed."

Jim looked straight at Peter and snapped, "Well maybe it has, but not without good reason. You don't know the people I have to work with! They're all a bunch of idiots."

"I don't need to know the people you work with. I know you."

"And what's *that* supposed to mean?" He practically spit the words at his friend.

Miller saw the twitching at the corner of Manion's jaw. "Not what you think it means." He continued, "Do you own a video camera?"

"What's that got to do with anything?"

"Just answer the question."

"Yes, I have a video camera. So what?"

"Do you ever use the pause button?"

Jim Manion rolled his eyes. "Yes, I've used the pause button. Listen, I didn't come here for a lesson on how to use a video camera."

"When you use the pause button, it freezes a scene, right?"

Manion nodded his agreement.

"It's the same with how we all see the world. Sometimes we get stuck in 'freeze-frame.' We get locked on to a certain perspective about an issue, a person, a job, whatever, . . . and we can't seem to advance the image."

We get stuck in "freeze-frame." We get locked on to a certain perspective about an issue, a person, a job.

"So?"

"So, when we freeze the frame on something, we sometimes freeze it on a bad spot. A bad perspective causes bad things to happen."

"I see where this is leading. Next you're going to tell me this entire thing is my fault!"

"I'd prefer to use the word *responsibility* over fault."

"Well, thanks for your support."

Miller glanced at Manion then opened a drawer in his desk and rummaged through some papers. "Jim, we've been friends for a long time. Would you do three things for me if I asked you to?"

Manion glared at Peter Miller then closed his eyes and took a deep breath. "I suppose so."

"Good." Miller took out some sheets of blank paper and a stack of envelopes from his desk drawer. "I want you to make up a page for each of the people that is on this management committee you've been telling me about. Next I want you to take about two minutes for each person and write down the adjectives you feel best describe each one."

"That's it?"

"No, after you're done, put each sheet in an envelope marked with that person's name. Then seal the envelopes."

"Got a pen?" asked Manion. Peter flipped one to Jim and

quietly left the room. Manion spent the next fifteen minutes doing the exercise just as Miller had instructed. Peter reentered the room just as Manion was finishing up the last sheet.

"OK, so much for the first request. There's two more things I'd like you to do," Miller said to Manion. "First, think about a time when you were involved in a really heated argument, preferably with someone Karen has never met. Someone she's never even heard of, and a situation you've never told her about. Got one?"

Jim sat silently for a few minutes. "OK, I've got a person and a situation in mind."

"Describe it to me."

"A few years back, when I was at the previous company, we were trying to set up our own in-house advertising agency. Things were going really well with our negotiations with the media until we hit one particular publisher. The guy just wouldn't buy into what we were trying to do. I just couldn't get him to give our company the 15 percent discount we were after. I ended up really blowing a gasket and threatening to pull all our advertising dollars if the publication didn't play ball. We eventually got our way, but the negotiations took so long it set us back a whole year. It was pretty ugly for a while."

Peter Miller smiled. "The next thing I'd like you to do is write an overview of the situation describing what you were trying to accomplish and the role of the publisher. Don't include any reference about the personalities involved, the tone of the negotiations, or the outcome. Now for the last thing I want you to do. When you get home I want you to ask Karen to play the role of the publisher. Give her the overview to read so she'll understand her role, then act out the scenario as if it were real life. Keep clear in your mind that it's not Karen you're speaking to, but that same publisher from the past."

"And how is this little game going to help me?"

"You'll discover that for yourself," said Miller. "Make sure you ask Karen for her reactions to the role-playing. Since she knows you best, her insights will be very valuable to you. Give me a call in the morning so we can discuss it. Ten o'clock would be good for me."

The two friends shook hands. Jim Manion walked out the door with seven sealed envelopes in hand, the written overview, and a commitment to role-play with Karen.

4

IT WAS JUST AFTER SEVEN-THIRTY WHEN JIM MANION
pulled his car into the driveway. His mind had been racing
since he left Peter Miller's office. "First my boss, and now
even my best friend thinks I'm screwing up! You work your
tail off . . . for what? So people can dump on you? What are
you supposed to do? Be a simpleminded gopher? You speak
your mind, and you get crucified for it. All they want is an
imbecile to follow them around—a pull toy. Maybe I should
tie a rope around my waist, wear roller skates, and nod my
head, like one of those stupid dogs you used to see in the
rear window of teenagers' cars."

Manion stopped his train of thought. "Listen to me.
Who's kidding whom? I could never do that. Who needs a
life full of B.S. anyway? Maybe I should find something else
to do. Have my own business. There must be government
loans."

Manion turned off the engine, picked up his stack of envelopes, and locked the car. Lucky he'd called Karen that
morning and let her know about his meeting with Miller.
No point making the family hold up dinner for him.

"Working late again, Dad?" Jennifer greeted him with a
hug and a kiss.

"Nope. I was visiting with my friend Peter."

"Mom said you'd be late. Can you play with us to-night?"

"Sure, just give me a couple of minutes to change and grab something to eat. What do you want to do?"

"How 'bout playing Monopoly?"

"How about a game that doesn't take so long? It's getting late. Mom's not going to want you kids staying up late again tonight."

"OK, what about that card game with the plastic chips . . . Rummoli?" asked Jennifer.

"Sure. You go set it up in the dining room. Ask your brother if he wants to play too."

Jennifer scampered off to set up the game. Jim gave Karen a hug as he walked into the kitchen.

"How did your meeting with Peter go?" she asked.

"OK. Can we talk about it after the kids are in bed? Jennifer and Bryan want to play a game. I told them we could play Rummoli. Want to join us?"

"Sure, why don't you go and change. I'll warm something up for you in the microwave."

Jim changed quickly, took out some clothes for the next morning, then wolfed down his dinner. Jennifer set up the Rummoli mat and divided up the colored poker chips while Bryan shuffled the cards. Soon Jim and Karen joined the children at the dining room table and the game began.

The children squealed with delight when Karen tallied up the poker chips and announced that Jennifer and Bryan had the highest scores. After putting away the game board, Karen put the children to bed while Jim made his customary pot of evening coffee.

"Mmmm, coffee smells good," Karen said as she entered the kitchen. "So . . . let's have all the gory little details about your meeting with Peter."

"You don't beat around the bush, do you?"

"No, I'm a woman with a mission."

"I see. Now I'm a personal reclamation project for you too. Maybe I should take up drinking so I can make the folks at AA feel worthwhile."

Karen paused then decided to ignore Jim's comment. "Would you like cream and sugar for your coffee?"

"Yes, thank you. I didn't mean to snap. That last comment wasn't fair. I'm just feeling the stress of the situation."

"I know. Do you want to talk about your meeting with Peter?"

"It was one of the strangest talks we've ever had. I guess I was expecting that we'd focus on my discussion with Katherine Fisher. Instead we rambled off in a dozen directions, talking about stuff that didn't seem to have anything to do with the matter at hand. I'd bring us back to the situation at work, and we'd start a pretty serious discussion about it. But after a minute or two Peter would change the subject on me again. It was pretty frustrating for a while."

"Did you get anywhere?"

"Actually we did . . . at the end. Peter talked about relationships. Basically, he told me that if I wasn't getting along at work, it was my fault. Sorry—he said it was my *responsibility*. He went into this analogy about a video camera and how the way we perceive things determines the outcome of a situation."

---

*T*he way we perceive things determines the outcome of a situation.

"That makes some sense, hon. I see that a lot in some of the cases my firm deals with, especially with marriage breakups. You can tell right from the start which ones are going to be ugly, knock-down-drag-out fights, and which ones will stay pretty calm and civil."

"I suppose so. Anyway, Peter also had me write down some descriptions of the other members of the management committee. I guess he'll tell me what to do with them at some point. And I've got some homework to do . . . with you."

"Knowing Peter, that could be interesting."

"Actually, it's a role-playing exercise."

"Now you've piqued my interest."

"Don't get your hopes up. You're supposed to pretend to be a publisher I had some dealings with at the last company."

"What kind of publisher—trashy novels, or worse?"

Manion laughed at his wife. "Not quite. Can't you be serious for just a minute?"

"No, and it's one of the reasons you love me," Karen replied. "So tell me more about this little game of Peter's."

Jim handed Karen the outline he had prepared about his negotiation with the recalcitrant publisher. "You're supposed to take a few minutes to read this to get an understanding about the role-playing. When you're ready, I'll start. Just pretend you're the publisher and react normally to me. We'll role-play as if it were a telephone conversation, not a personal meeting."

Karen took the outline and walked into the adjoining family room. She sat on the chair facing the kitchen, looked at the instructions for a few minutes, then turned to her husband, ready to start.

Jim began the exchange from his seat at the kitchen table. "Hello, Mr. Gibson, this is Jim Manion calling."

"Good morning, Mr. Manion. What can I do for you today?" Karen replied in a direct and businesslike manner.

"Mr. Gibson, as you may be aware, our company is planning to set up an in-house advertising agency. We're approaching all the publications we've dealt with in the past to make the necessary arrangements."

"Specifically, what kind of arrangements are you looking to set up, Mr. Manion?"

"We hope that all the publications will treat our in-house staff as a regular advertising agency. We want to negotiate directly with each publication and take the standard 15 percent agency commission off the rates we negotiate. There won't be any negative impact to your bottom line since you're already giving away the 15 percent now anyway. In fact, you should be able to be more profitable under this scenario since you won't have to duplicate your sales efforts by calling on our advertising agency as well as our people." Manion felt comfortable with the pitch he was giving Karen. After all, he had had the same kind of conversation with dozens of publishers.

"We appreciate your goal, Mr. Manion, but what you're asking for goes against our standard policy. We get a fair amount of our revenue through advertising agency contacts," Karen countered.

"We're not all that interested in outdated policies, Mr. Gibson. We've had no difficulty with the other publishers we've spoken to."

Karen looked at Jim for a moment, then replied, "What other publishers choose to do is their business, Mr. Manion. I'm not sure I agree that our publication would be more profitable dealing with you directly. We still have to make agency contacts, perhaps not on your account, but there are overheads that still need to be covered. . . ."

Manion interrupted Karen. "Why should my company pay for overheads we don't need? That doesn't make good business sense. If some of your other clients want the added expense of dealing through an advertising agency, that's their decision, not ours. Your publication needs to get out of the dark ages and deal with the realities of doing business today."

"As I said earlier, Mr. Manion, as a publisher I need to look at our fixed marketing costs, regardless of how advertising is purchased."

"Well, I can give you a choice that's pretty simple, Mr. Gibson. Would you rather stick to your guns and hold onto an extra 15 percent of nothing, or give my company the 15 percent agency discount direct and get some advertising from us?"

"Why are you doing this?" Karen asked.

"Well, it's pretty simple, Mr. Gibson. . . . "

This time it was Karen interrupting her husband. "Jim, why are you jumping down my throat when I'm trying to help you?"

"Help me! You're trying to screw my company by forcing me to pay an extra 15 percent I shouldn't have to pay."

"I was just trying to understand the situation a little more fully and get you to see my perspective. I was actually working the game toward offering you a 10 percent discount," Karen explained.

"Ten percent! I told you the deal was for 15 percent."

"Karen Okira calling Jim Manion . . . Karen Okira calling Jim Manion. Come in Jim Manion."

Manion stopped dead and looked at his wife. "OK, what's your point?" he asked.

"Since we started the role-playing you haven't listened to a word I've said," replied Karen. "I've never known you to be this aggressive. Bullish."

"Look, it's just a game. I didn't mean anything by it. Don't take it personally."

"What happened when you dealt with the real Mr. Gibson?"

"We got into a big fracas. He drew a line in the sand and wouldn't give us the agency discount. It ended up that I had to get a media buying service to purchase the space for me on a reduced commission basis. We got a rebate of 11 percent from them, so it really only cost us 4 percentage points.

Eventually we got the situation turned around, and we got Gibson's publication to give us the 15 percent, but it took us a year to do it. You know, when I think about it, it still makes my blood boil. We wasted a whole year, and it cost us four points more than it should have for that one year."

Karen looked Jim straight in the eye. "I'm surprised he gave you anything. Are you always such a rotten SOB to deal with?"

Manion chuckled. "Sometimes you have to be a little tough. Enough's enough. Let's forget about this stupid game."

"You still don't get it, do you, Jim?" Karen asked. "I became Gibson in that role-playing. I mean, I really became him in your mind, and you treated me the exact way you treated him."

"Of course I did. You were supposed to be Gibson in the role-playing. Who else was I supposed to treat you like?" quipped Manion.

"But the reality of the game was that I was a different Mr. Gibson. I didn't know very much about the real Gibson, did I? I didn't have any clue about what kind of relationship you had with him or what kind of person he was. I had no idea that he originally refused to give you the deal. I was playing him from my perspective. I was trying to keep you as a customer and find some middle ground so we'd both be happy, but you refused to listen. I realized pretty quickly that there was nothing I could do to change the outcome. You were determined to force me into a corner. You wanted to play chicken and see who would blink first."

Jim Manion held his wife's gaze for a few moments then looked down at his coffee cup. "Come on, it's only a game. There's no sense fighting over something so trivial."

Karen took a few sips of her coffee. She picked up a magazine from the end table and casually thumbed through it for a few moments. "Before we drop the issue, I'd like you to answer one final question about the game. Did our role-playing parallel what happened in real life with Gibson?"

Manion kept his gaze fixed on the top of the kitchen table, the fingers of his right hand gently traced the pattern of the wood grain. He bit his lower lip as he looked into the family room at Karen. His answer was a simple yes.

Karen put the magazine down and walked into the kitchen. She put her arms around Manion and held him close to her. "Call Peter in the morning. Come on, it's getting late. Let's go to bed."

5

KATHERINE FISHER WAS IN THE OFFICE EARLY ON FRIDAY. Recurring thoughts about her conversation with Philippe Fontaine had kept her tossing and turning most of the night. She couldn't shake what he'd said. "Katherine, if we really want to turn this situation around, we need to look for environmental factors that could have contributed to Manion's abrasiveness. Did your attitude and reactions to him change before the new behavior started?"

During the meeting she had completely dismissed that possibility. Now that she'd had some time to think about it she wasn't so sure. Fisher knew that Jim Manion was a little delicate to handle. He was a marketing vice president and a highly creative and task-oriented person with a natural inclination toward dominant behavior. But only under extreme stress did traces of it start to show. Manion seemed to understand this trait in himself, and almost without exception he had been successful in controlling his behavior. In the past Katherine had been careful to watch for early warning signs, and she usually adjusted her interactions with Manion accordingly. Lately, she thought, her compensating didn't make any difference in Jim's behavior.

Fisher was very concerned that Manion's aggressiveness

and uncooperative attitude toward the other members of the team was starting to fracture the organization. She was also well aware of his talents and was equally afraid of losing him. Manion had brought excellent project management skills to the organization along with his marketing expertise. The marketing department was much more focused and results oriented under his leadership, and as a result the company had gained 4 percentage points in market share during the first three years of his tenure, much of it traceable to improved returns on direct marketing initiatives he had developed.

Fisher had relived the meeting with Fontaine during her drive to work. She vividly recalled the flinch Philippe registered when she asked him what a severance package for Manion might cost. And when Fontaine had suggested documenting the situation as per company policy, she had declined. Katherine wondered if her instincts were at work. Was something inside her trying to get her to realize that she bore some of the responsibility for Manion's behavior?

Sitting behind her gleaming rosewood desk, Katherine set out her priorities for the day and tried to erase the subject from her mind. "At least Philippe will be seeing Manion next Tuesday. He'll report back on Jim's reaction and the likelihood that the situation can be salvaged. At any rate, it will be over in three months one way or another."

On the other side of the building Jim Manion was also in early and planning his day. In his case, the planning focused on making sure that nothing would interfere with the call he planned to make to Peter Miller at ten o'clock.

"Peter was right about the role-playing with Karen," thought Manion. "The fact that the make-believe negotiation with her turned ugly just like it had with Gibson proved that my perceptions had a huge impact on the outcome. I wonder what he has up his sleeve next? Maybe he'll tell me what to do with those envelopes today. I've got to try to get my head together for my meeting with Fontaine next week."

After he organized a dozen files, Manion dug in his heels and started his workday. He ripped through four of the files quickly. At nine-forty-five he put his telephone on call forward. There was no way he could wait until ten o'clock to call Miller.

"Peter, I was hoping I could catch you before ten," Manion greeted his friend.

"I expected you'd call early. How did it go last night with Karen?"

"She had her analytic tools out. I escaped a full-blown cross-examination, but she made her points nonetheless."

"What did she say?"

"Basically, she got me to agree that I had treated her just like the real Mr. Gibson. I really got into the role-playing . . . maybe carried away a bit. She was shocked by my aggressiveness. She said she had never seen the bully side of me before. It really hit home. I certainly never thought of myself as the bully type before."

"Don't sweat it, Jim. All of us get out of touch with ourselves at times. It's one of life's great pleasures."

"Pleasures?"

"Sure, whenever you realize that you're operating outside the person you've defined yourself to be, it's a golden opportunity for self-discovery. There's no lesson in life more important."

Whenever you realize that you're operating outside the person you've defined yourself to be, it's a golden opportunity for self-discovery.

"So where do we go from here, Peter?"

"Did you bring the envelopes to work with you?"

"No, I left them at home."

"That's good. I wouldn't want to put more temptation in front of you than you could handle. What I'd like you to do is pull out seven blank sheets of paper, one for each member of the management committee. Then write down adjectives that describe the relationship you have with each of those individuals. Put each in a separate envelope, then label the envelope with the person's name and seal it, just like you did with the first exercise. What's on for the weekend?"

"Nothing much, really. Karen wants to take the children out to the community center about ten o'clock Saturday morning. She's signing them up for art classes. That won't take more than an hour. Other than that we'll be around all weekend."

"I'll give you a call early tomorrow morning so we can confirm a time to meet. I want to come over Saturday afternoon so we can discuss the contents of those envelopes."

"I'll save you a call. Let's make it two o'clock. I was wondering when we'd get to the envelopes. Any hints?"

Peter chuckled. "You should know me better than that, Jim. Knowledge is like fine wine. It shouldn't be opened before its time. What's your fax number at the office? I want to send you an article to read over before I see you tomorrow."

Manion gave Miller his fax number and then walked over to the fax machine in the marketing department. "You never know what he's likely to send," thought Manion. "It's probably a good idea to be here to receive it firsthand." Within thirty seconds a fax cover sheet from Peter's office started to emerge from the machine. It was followed by a newspaper clipping, its heading: UPROAR OVER CRIME TATTOOS IN INDIA. Jim picked up the article and scanned it briefly. "What the devil has this got to do with anything?" he wondered.

Back in his office, Manion sat down and read the first portion of the article.

UPROAR OVER CRIME TATTOOS IN INDIA

AMRITSAR, India. A national controversy has erupted in India's northern state of Punjab. Six women claim that vengeful police officers tattooed the word *pickpocket* on their foreheads to settle personal scores.

Police disputed the accusation stating that the women had been tattooed by their own neighbors as a warning to others.

The incident has raised serious questions about police conduct and how far authorities should be allowed to go to control crime.

"Peter . . . Peter . . . Peter," thought Manion. "What am I supposed to do with this?" He put the article in his brief-case and made a note to himself to show it to Karen when he got home.

Then he took his telephone off call forward and tackled some more of the files piled around him.

Just before noon Jim stopped working so he could figure out the best place to have something to eat and work on his latest exercise from Peter. He decided on a small Italian res-taurant that had three definite advantages: the pasta was good and reasonably priced, there were some private booths toward the back of the room, and very few people from the office went there to eat. Manion put the seven blank sheets of paper and the accompanying envelopes in a file folder and left for lunch.

The restaurant was situated in a strip mall about four blocks from the office. Jim was a regular customer and got a warm greeting from the owners. There was no problem get-ting one of the private booths at the back of the room. He or-dered the special of the day: calamari and spaghetti with meat sauce and a small salad.

To begin the new exercise Peter had assigned him, Man-ion thought about how he would describe his relationship with each of the members of the management committee in turn. He then put pen to paper, and soon a stream of adjectives was flowing. Soon his lunch arrived, and he was enjoying his calamari and writing at the same time. As he completed each sheet, he labelled the top of the page with the name of the committee member, folded it, and placed it in an envelope. Within fifteen minutes he had completed the exercise. "That was pretty easy," he thought. "Somehow I don't think tomorrow will be quite as simple."

Rush-hour traffic was a little lighter than usual that evening. Jim arrived home just after six o'clock in good spirits. The meeting with Katherine Fisher earlier in the week had served as a catalyst. Manion couldn't remember the last time he had had a more productive week. "If I put enough weeks like this together, there's no way they'll be able to afford to cut me loose," he thought.

Karen greeted him at the front door. "Ready for the weekend?"

"You bet. I spoke to Peter today. He's coming over tomorrow afternoon around two to discuss the two envelope exercises he gave me."

"Two exercises? When did you get the other one?"

"This morning when I called him at the office. I had to describe my relationship with each of the committee members. Didn't take too long to do." Jim opened his briefcase. "Peter faxed me the strangest newspaper clipping."

He handed Karen the fax. She looked at the heading. "Has Peter been smoking his old gym socks? What's this got to do with you?"

"I have no idea. But Peter said he wanted me to read the article before he came over tomorrow. We should plan to have him stay for dinner. How about homemade pizza? The kids always get a charge out of that."

"Sure, I can ask them what kind of toppings they want. What do you think Peter will like?"

"Who knows. Let's buy some really weird stuff and see what he does."

Karen laughed. "Leave it to me. Mr. Miller will be in for a real culinary treat!"

The Manions pitched in to prepare dinner. By six-thirty the family was gathered around the kitchen table. Discussion was lively. The children were especially talkative, volunteering numerous details about the day's activities. Jim picked up a salt shaker and pretended it was a microphone. The children howled as he conducted mock interviews with them.

After the children were in bed, Manion prepared another pot of coffee. As he waited for it to brew, he picked up the faxed newspaper clipping and read it through. "This is a really bizarre story," he said to Karen. "I can't believe people would physically label other people. Imagine, they tattooed the word *jebkatri* right on the foreheads of these six women."

"What does it mean?" Karen asked.

"Pickpocket."

"Pickpocket?"

Jim nodded his head.

"If I was going to be labelled for the rest of my life, I suppose I'd want to commit a crime a little more serious, or at least more fun," Karen said. She took the article from Jim and read it over. "Peter obviously thinks it's relevant to your situation, but for the life of me I can't see how tattooing women in India has anything to do with you."

Manion poured two cups of coffee and handed one to Karen. "Well, that's Peter for you. He's abstract. He's eccentric, . . . bizarre, odd, quirky, but he's also smart. It means something."

6

Saturday morning felt like it lasted a month. Jim had been pacing around the house for hours, unable to separate his feelings of anticipation from trepidation. The children sensed his tension and gave him a wide berth.

It was about ten after two when Manion finally saw Peter Miller's car pull into the driveway and lurch to a halt. Files in hand, Miller strode up the driveway.

"Hello Peter, come on in," Manion greeted his friend. "Can you stay for dinner?"

"As long as you're not cooking, I'll definitely consider it," Peter replied.

After exchanging greetings with Karen and the children, Peter followed Manion into the living room.

"Figured we'd have less noise and interruptions in here," Jim continued. "I have a meeting with HR on Tuesday next week." He glanced nervously at the two stacks of envelopes on the coffee table.

"So where's my cup of coffee?" was Miller's reply. "It's bad enough I'm treating you like a charity case, charging no fee. I'm not going to let you get away with skimping on the refreshments."

"How thirsty are you? Will a cup of instant do, or should we make a pot?"

Miller's hand covered his heart. "Instant? You expect me to drink instant? Has our relationship deteriorated to that extent? I'm cut to the quick."

Manion laughed, "Alright, let's go into the kitchen and we'll get a pot brewing. You shrink types are all so temperamental." Soon the smell of fresh coffee filled the room.

"When are you going to buy a new car, Peter? You've had the same one ever since I've known you. It's got to be twelve years old by now."

"Nearly thirteen and a half if the truth be known. I suppose I'll get rid of it when I need a new one."

"Body's pretty rusted. How much do you have on it?"

"One hundred and eighty-three thousand miles."

"One hundred and eighty-three thousand and you don't think you need a new car?"

"It gets me from A to B in relative comfort and style."

"Comfort and style! Come on, Peter, you've used so much body filler on it, I'll bet we couldn't find half a dozen places on the whole car where a magnet would stick!"

"Maybe so. What's on the surface isn't important to me. The real value is what's underneath."

"There's probably just more rust."

"It runs like a top," said Miller. "I've never missed an oil change or filter change. Done all the prescribed maintenance. You can patch up almost any external blemish as long as what's inside has been properly looked after."

You can patch up almost any external blemish as long as what's inside has been properly looked after.

Jim gave Miller a quick glance and smiled. "So how long are you going to keep it?"

"Until I need a new one."

"Let's go into the living room. This discussion is going nowhere fast."

The two men sat across from one another at the coffee table. Peter took some papers out of one of his file folders. "Let's jump right into this. I've brought a simple behavior assessment I want you to do. It's called the Personal Profile System. Have you ever done one before?" Miller handed it to Manion.

Jim looked over the form. "Not personally, but a lot of my friends have done it," he answered.

"So you're comfortable with it and its level of accuracy?"

"Yeah. I remember my friends saying they were amazed at how well it nailed them down."

"Before we get into the envelopes, I want you to do the assessment three times. As you do each assessment I want you to think about a different member of the management committee and mark the form based on how you act with that individual."

"Three times? You don't want me to do one for each member of the committee?"

"If we had more time you could. What I really want to do is simply illustrate a concept with you, so three should be enough. This will work best if you pick someone you've got a good relationship with, another one you have a poor relationship with, and a third that's best described as average."

"Do I have to tell you who upfront?"

"Nope. Just make a note on each form so we can tell them apart later. It shouldn't take you more than twenty minutes to do the three assessments. I'll go chat with Karen until you're done."

Jim examined the first assessment. There were twenty-eight different groupings of four words each. All he had to do was identify which word in each grouping was most like him and which was the least like him. After working on the forms for about fifteen minutes, Manion glanced toward the doorway and caught Miller peeking around the corner.

"How are you doing?"

"Just finishing up the last one. Another couple of minutes should do it."

Miller walked into the living room and picked up the coffee mugs. "I'll make like the host and get us each a fresh cup."

Peter returned with fresh coffee and explained how to score and interpret the material. After scoring and graphing the results of the three assessments, Peter handed them to Manion, saying, "Let's key in on graph number three since it's the one that assesses your behavior based on both your self-perception and your perception of the environment around you. If the theory holds true, we should find that graph number three changes as your perception of your environment changes."

"So I could view this graph as identifying the behavior that I'm likely to exhibit around a particular individual in my environment, and that's why we'd see changes?"

"Exactly."

Jim stared at the graphs in apparent disbelief.

"Look at this, Peter! The curves are all different!"

"Ah, the wonder of modern science."

Jim studied the instructions on the form. "So now we compare the shape of the curves with the classic profile descriptions, right?"

"Jim, you've underestimated yourself all these years. You do have more than a couple of live brain cells."

Manion compared his graphs with the standard curves. "This one says I'm a Creative."

"That shouldn't be a surprise. After all, you've been in marketing most of your career," Miller replied.

Manion studied the description of his basic behavior traits. "This is incredible. It's almost as if they used me as a model when they came up with this classification."

Manion checked his scores for the other two assessments, then reviewed the classic behavior descriptions for each. "Looks like I'm schizophrenic, or at the very least one of my ancestors must have mated with a chameleon. Talk about all over the map!"

"Your charts are more diverse than average, Jim, but having a wide spread isn't that unusual. It just means that you perceive that your work environment demands a range of different behaviors. Remember when I asked you to think about a specific management committee member when you did each form?"

Manion nodded.

Peter continued, "Framing each of the assessments in terms of your relationship with individual members of the management committee enabled it to pick up the differences in your behavior. It really drives home the point that how you perceive each person has a definite impact on the way you choose to deal with them."

Miller picked up one of the forms and studied it intently for a few minutes. "Who did you have in mind when you did this one?"

"Lynne."

"Open up the envelopes with her name on them and compare the description you wrote of her, your relationship with her, and the behavior style on this form."

Jim placed the three documents alongside one another and examined them. After a few minutes he looked up at Miller. "This is starting to make sense. Since Lynne is autocratic, dictatorial, and aggressive, I perceive her that way, and in order to be effective with her, I fight fire with fire by dealing with her in a very direct, bottom-line manner: the results-oriented style." Manion appeared confident in his interpretation.

"Do you have a copy of the article I faxed to your office?" asked Peter.

"I gave it to Karen when I got home last night. Let me see where she put it. We both thought it was pretty weird."

Manion left for the kitchen and reappeared in a few minutes, article in hand. "Here it is, Peter. I've got to admit that I don't see what tattooing the foreheads of women in India has to do with me."

"We may not tattoo people physically as this article describes, but we label people and ourselves all the time. Lynne isn't autocratic, dictatorial, or aggressive except in your mind. Your perception of her comes first. It determines what style you use in dealing with her. As you said, you choose a no-nonsense, bottom-line approach with her, the results-oriented style, which is characterized by high amounts of dominant behavior patterns and is very confrontational. The way you choose to behave with her then causes her to react to you in a dictatorial and aggressive fashion."

"I don't see it that way at all," countered Manion. "The way I figure it, she is, so I do."

"Is that how the role-playing worked with Karen?"

Jim's mind flashed back to the role-playing. He remembered the looks Karen gave him during the game, and her interpretation of what had happened.

Peter continued, "Do you remember the comedian Flip Wilson? Geraldine was one of the characters he created for his act. She was a pretty fiery, and shall we say, a somewhat lusty character. Geraldine had a few pet phrases. One of them was "What you see is what you get, honey!"

Miller held up the sheet of adjectives Jim had written to describe Lynne. "This is how you see Lynne. As a result of how you see her, you choose to respond to her in ways that will make your interpretation of her a reality. What you see is what you get!"

"Now you're blaming me for how she acts?"

"I'm not talking about blaming anyone."

"Excuse me, but she's an adult and as such is supposed to be responsible for her behavior. You can't hold me accountable for her actions."

"I'm not trying to. I just want you to realize that you are accountable for how you see and interpret the world around you."

> ### You are accountable for how you see and interpret the world around you.

"Listen, like I said, I perceive and react to Lynne based on the things she does to me."

"No, my friend, you don't. You perceive her based on how you *interpret* what she does. What she does is simply what she does, an event. How you process that event makes it good or bad."

"Come on, Peter! Are you trying to tell me that everyone's actions are ethical and well intended?"

"Absolutely not. There are some unscrupulous characters out there. But that's no excuse for us to make assumptions about people, either good or bad."

"So what are we supposed to do?"

"We need to suspend our judgment and play the role of an impartial observer, that way we learn someone's true nature and how to deal with them."

"I'm still not sure I buy that."

Miller paused and studied his friend. "Let me ask you a question. Was the signing of the NAFTA agreement good or bad for our economy?"

"Bad. It will cause jobs to move to Mexico where the labor rates are lower. It will cause working conditions to erode and employee benefits to be reduced. There will be a net loss of jobs here, higher unemployment, followed by higher taxes to support the growing number of jobless."

"But that's not what many high-profile business leaders say about the deal. They support it. They say it will be good for our economy. It will open up new markets and create jobs and wealth here."

"They're probably in business segments that won't feel the same kind of competitive pressures my company faces."

"So who's right?" Peter asked.

"I guess time will tell."

"What happens if some companies in your industry lose jobs as you predict, and other companies in your industry grow as some business leaders say they will? Who will be right then?"

"Depends on your point of view."

"That's all I've been trying to say, Jim. NAFTA is a trade treaty. An event. How we interpret it makes it good or bad in our minds. Our interpretation is based on our perceptions."

Manion sat motionless on the sofa. "Let me see that sheet about Lynne again," he said, taking the paper from Peter's hand. "So what you're getting at is that Lynne is a person. Not a good person or a bad person. Just a person. And you're saying that I define her as bad based on how I interpret her actions."

"That's right."

"Sounds too simplistic to me. There are people out there who will do anything to get ahead. Are you saying that I should automatically trust everyone until they stab me in the back?" asked Jim.

"That's not what I'm saying at all. Trust is something that has to be earned over time. What I'm suggesting is that we should observe the actions of other people objectively, and not jump to any immediate conclusions. Maintaining an impartial viewpoint allows us to accurately discover someone's true nature without having to pass judgment on them."

"But, we still may find out that we're dealing with someone who has no ethics or morals."

"Absolutely. There are destructive personalities out there that we need to be very cautious around, but let's not have a negative view of everyone."

"So, you're saying that I could misinterpret some of Lynne's actions, and as a result, think of her as my enemy."

"Exactly. And, how you define her determines what kind of behavior you exhibit toward her, which in turn creates your relationship," explained Peter.

"She must do the same thing. She must define me."

"Sure she does." Miller picked up the newspaper clipping he had faxed to Jim. "It's like these women in India who had their foreheads tattooed because they were pickpockets. All of us do the same kind of thing all the time. We don't tattoo people, but we do label them. Then whenever we see them, we immediately call up the labels we've put on them, and we respond accordingly. It really doesn't give the other person much of a chance to show us other parts of their personality. Once you or Lynne define one another in negative terms, you'll react to each other in ways that will create a negative relationship. The brain follows a natural process to prove that the original judgments it made were correct."

***O**nce you define someone in negative terms, you'll react to him or her in ways that will create a negative relationship.*

"I'm sure she feels as negative about me as I do about her. How do I get her to change?"

"You can't. She is what she is. In fact, the root of most personal conflict stems from one person trying to make another person change. It's like the disillusionment stage in marriage. After the honeymoon is over, somewhere between three weeks and three years after the wedding, you realize your mate doesn't fit the ideal you had in your head when you got married. What normally happens is each of the partners tries to change the other one to fit his or her original expectations. It creates a tremendous amount of conflict and dissatisfaction within the marriage. I think it's the primary cause of the seven-year itch."

The root of most personal conflict stems from one person trying to make another person change.

"So if I can't change her, what can I do?"

"Change your perception of her."

"And that's supposed to enable me to change my behavior around her, which in turn will help change our relationship into a positive one?"

"Absolutely. Remember when we talked about the pause button on a video camera? When you use that button, you freeze the scene. It's the same with our perceptions of other people. If we currently have a negative perception of someone, we need to advance the tape so we can focus on the positive traits. Otherwise there is no hope of changing our view of the other person. Read some of the traits you used to describe Lynne."

Manion scanned the list. "Negative. Problem-oriented. Picky. Blunt."

Peter interrupted him. "Just in those opening comments there are some positives you can build on!"

Manion looked puzzled.

Miller continued, "When you're developing a plan, it's important to have someone look at it with a critical eye to evaluate where things could go wrong. You could be too close to the project to see some things that might be obvious to others. Lynne could be an important ally. It's a simple matter of changing the labels you put on her. Change "negative" and "problem-oriented" to "pragmatic" and "realistic." Choose to call her detail-oriented rather than picky. Call her candid, a straight shooter, rather than blunt. She still may do the same thing, but by altering your choice of words, you improve your view of her. You start to turn what you perceived as her weaknesses into strengths."

"You're right. I just never thought about it quite like that before. It puts the role-playing with Karen in perspective. I had a negative view of the publisher, and I transferred that perception to her. We ended up acting out what was in my head. It wasn't Karen or Gibson. . . . It was me, and the more I think about the situation at work, it's the same with Lynne. She's always brought her analytic, objective views to the table. I'm just not accepting them the way I used to."

"How so?"

"I remember the first year I was at the company. She took me aside and explained some of the problems that manufacturing was going to have trying to build one of the new products I was responsible for launching. I accepted her input more openly then, and we discussed her concerns in detail. We solved the problems for manufacturing, and we also found some cost savings that we could pass along to our customers. It made us even more competitive in the market, and sales went way beyond expectations, which made me look like a star. I wrote a memo to Fisher to make sure Lynne got the credit she deserved for her input." Manion shook his head. "Lynne and I used to get along great until the last year or so."

Peter looked at Jim and smiled. "Excuse me for a second." He got up and went to the hall closet. After rummaging through the pockets in his jacket, Miller returned to the living room and handed Manion a four-inch-long stainless-steel bolt. "I was hoping I could give you this today."

Jim put his hand over his heart. "Oh Peter, you shouldn't have! What I've always wanted . . . an adult-size Meccano set! It must be part of one of those incredible TV offers."

Manion cupped his left hand over his ear, lowered his voice to a mock announcer tone. "Friends, this is truly a once-in-a-lifetime opportunity. For only twelve easy payments of twenty-nine ninety-five you too can build this one-forty-second-scale replica of the Eiffel Tower. Call the number on your screen now! All major credit cards accepted."

The men shared a hearty laugh.

"So, Peter, what's really the point of the bolt?"

"Now that you've insulted my gift, you don't really expect me to tell you, do you?"

"Well, at least give me a hint."

"Let's get the rest of our work done first. We've got all the other envelopes to go through. We need to examine each sheet of adjectives and rework as many of the negatives into positives as we can. We'll need to do the same thing with the sheets that describe your current relationships. Then the real fun will begin."

7

THE BACON SIZZLED IN THE PAN AS KAREN HUMMED THE chorus of one of her favorite oldies tunes. Peter Miller had left late the previous evening. It was a little after two when Jim came upstairs, and Karen knew he would be tired this morning. She had decided before going to bed the previous night that she was going to make him breakfast in bed.

When the pancakes were done, she placed them carefully on a plate on the bed tray then slowly climbed the stairs to the master bedroom. She placed the tray on the floor and sat on the edge of the bed, looking down at her sleeping husband. The same gentleness she had married fourteen years ago was still there. She stroked his hair and felt the sandpaper roughness of his unshaven face.

"Jim . . . Jim . . . time for breakfast." She cradled his head in her hands and kissed him on the forehead. Jim began to stir.

"Mornin'," he said with a yawn. Karen's face began to come into focus. She kissed him warmly.

"Made you breakfast. You were up pretty late last night working with Peter. Thought you could use a little TLC."

Jim propped his pillow against the headboard and sat up as Karen placed the tray in front of him.

"This looks wonderful! Are you going to eat?"

"I already had something with the kids. How did it go with Peter?"

"Great. What a fantastic guy," said Manion. "Imagine giving up a big hunk of your weekend to help a friend the way he did."

He started into his fruit salad. "We worked on some techniques I can use to turn this thing around. I think there's light at the end of the tunnel."

"That's good. What did you do?" Karen asked.

"Peter gave me some behavior assessments. He left a copy for you to work on if you're interested."

Balancing the breakfast tray, Jim reached down, grabbed a file from the floor next to the bed, and opened up an assessment. "It's really simple. You just go down these groupings of words and mark the one that best describes you and the word that's least like you. After you've finished all twenty-eight items, you just rub a coin over your selections, which causes a chemical reaction, and presto, the answer code appears. After scoring the form you match up the results with the Classical Profile Patterns at the back."

"So am I married to an axe murderer?"

"No, more like Dr. Jekyll and Mr. Hyde."

"Oh?"

"Peter had me do three separate assessments. I had to think about a different management committee member when I did each one. It was incredible how my behavior style changed depending on who I was thinking about. On one of them I was like Attila the Hun and Prince Charming on a different one. It was a real eye-opener."

"What did the behavior curves look like?"

Jim spread the three forms out for Karen to examine. "See, I'm like a chameleon. I exhibit a range of styles depending on who I'm dealing with. This is the behavior I exhibit with Lynne, this one with Katherine, and the last one with Wilkinson."

"What one are you with Katherine?"

"I'm a Creative."

"That makes sense."

"Don't be fooled by the name. You could be an accountant, lawyer, or engineer and still be a Creative. Here's a summary profile of the type." Jim opened the reference portion of the form and handed it to Karen.

He gobbled his pancakes as she started to read the description. She commented, "I see what you mean. This type certainly is you." Karen read from the text:

> Persons with the Creative Pattern display two opposite forces in their behavior. Desire for tangible accomplishments is counterbalanced by an equal striving for perfection. Aggressiveness is tempered with sensitivity. Quickness of thought and reaction time are restrained by the wish to explore all possible solutions before deciding.

"Look about halfway down the left-hand column," Jim directed.

"Where it says 'value to the organization'?"

"From that point down."

Karen read the headings and descriptions out loud. "Value to the organization . . . initiator or designer of changes. Overuses . . . bluntness . . . critical or condescending attitude. Under pressure . . . easily bored with routine work . . . sulky when unwillingly restrained . . . assertive and pioneering. Fears not being influential . . . failure to achieve their standards. Would increase effectiveness with more warmth . . . tactful communication . . . team cooperation . . . recognition that sanctions exist."

"I was thinking about that description during dinner last night."

"You were a little preoccupied."

"I couldn't help it. Doing the assessment really put Katherine Fisher's comments into sharp focus. It's like waking up the morning after a party when you've had too much to drink. You're in pain, real pain, and you want to blame somebody for how bad you feel. But deep down you know you've done it to yourself. When I think about what I've said to people lately and how I've treated them, I feel like such an ass."

"Don't be too rough on yourself," Karen said. "No one is perfect. We've all got warts. The assessment just proves that those traits are a natural part of your personality that you'll have to learn to deal with."

"That's no excuse. If you accept the negative parts of your personality as cast in stone, you'll never grow. It's like thinking that you're Popeye—the old 'I am what I am' syndrome."

If you accept the negative parts of your personality as cast in stone, you'll never grow.

"What does Peter think you need to do to turn things around?"

"Change the program," Jim replied.

Karen cocked her head to one side and looked intently at her husband. "Change what program?"

"My program. The one I create that makes me do what I do. Peter and I talked a lot about perceptions. Of ourselves. People around us. Our environment. The world. It's really amazing how our behavior is a direct result of how we see things around us. It's like that article Peter sent me about the six women who were tattooed in India."

"He was actually able to make sense out of that clipping for you?"

"Definitely. I never thought about it much before, but it's true: we constantly label ourselves and other people around us. Peter really drove the point home when he had me open up the envelopes."

"The ones that had the descriptions of the management committee members?"

"Uh-huh. Every one of those adjectives I wrote was a label I put on a particular person. Most of them weren't very complimentary. It was the same thing with the sheets where I described my work relationships. Most of the words I used were negative. Peter explained that once you put a label on someone or something, your brain does a scan looking for evidence to support your belief. When you put a negative label on someone, it's as if you tattooed that adjective on the person's forehead. Every time you are in contact with the person, you see that label. You act defensively because you expect the worst."

■

Once you put a label on someone or something, your brain goes on scan, looking for evidence to support your belief.

■

"And because you're uptight and defensive around them, they pick up on your reactions and are unable to act positively around you?" asked Karen.

"Exactly. When you have a negative perception about someone, that feeling ends up creating a negative relationship between the two of you. Depending on how ingrained your negative perception is, it can be as permanent as a tattoo. The key point Peter made was that the onus is on me to change my perceptions if I want my relationships to get better."

Jim ate the last piece of bacon and moved the bed tray
from his lap. He swung his legs over the side of the bed,
stood up, and stretched. Karen stood up beside him.

"Nice theory, . . . but how practical is it? I mean, if
someone at work is always chewing on you, how do you
suddenly get a warm, fuzzy feeling about them?" she asked.

"Peter talked about a phenomenon called freeze-frame.
He explained that if we freeze the frame on something negative, we need to advance the tape and focus on a more positive perspective. To be assured of a more positive outcome,
we need to suspend judgment on other people's actions. If
your boss is tearing a strip off you for no reason, rather than
take it as a negative personal experience, you could choose
to interpret your boss's actions as being out of character for
him or her. You may even choose to have sympathy for him
or her. After all, someone who behaves that way for no apparent reason must be deeply troubled."

Suspend judgment on the actions of other people.

"Unless you're a saint, I can't see anyone really doing
that."

"No one said it was going to be easy, but it's not as difficult as you may think." Jim padded over to his bureau and
pulled his jeans out of the bottom drawer. "We're condi-
tioned by our environment to focus on the downside of
most things, so we are predisposed to view events as negative," he said, threading his legs one by one into his blue
jeans. "The reality is that an event is just an event. It's how
we process it that makes it bad."

"I'm not sure that I agree. There are some things like

murder or a disaster like a plane crash that can't possibly be viewed as positive."

"Are you sure about that?"

"Yes, I can't see how either one could be perceived as positive."

Jim selected a T-shirt from the third bureau drawer. "Here's a couple for you. Imagine how many thousands of expatriate Cubans now living in Florida would be dancing in the streets of Miami if Fidel Castro were assassinated." He pulled the shirt over his head. "How many people in this country would think an airplane crash was good news if Qaddafi or Saddam Hussein were on it?"

"OK, maybe I'd agree with you in those unique situations, but you have to admit, you really had to stretch to come up with them."

"Of course I did. But the point is that if you can find a circumstance in which even murder may be perceived by some people as a positive event, then it stands to reason that our perceptions play a key role in our day-to-day lives. The circumstances surrounding an event are what really drive our perceptions. The event itself is secondary."

"Give me an example."

Jim thought for a moment then replied, "What would you think if you met an old friend on the street, and she told you that she just got a new job?"

"I'd think it was good news, of course."

"What if the last time you saw your friend she was a high-powered corporate lawyer making two hundred thousand a year, and the job she just got was as a short-order cook working the late-night shift at a burger joint?"

"Why's she in a burger joint?" asked Karen.

Manion smiled at his wife. "Trying to evaluate the circumstances, are we? That proves my point, you know."

"OK, it's bad. Something must have happened to her old position that has forced her into that kind of job. She's just there until she can find something else, and being on the night shift gives her time to work on her career search during the day."

"Let's say that she did lose her corporate job, and she's working in the burger joint to learn the ropes of the fast-food business before she buys into a couple of franchises."

"Then the job is obviously good, because it gives her more of an opportunity to investigate her potential investment." Karen nodded her head. "OK, you've made your point. I see how we judge events as good or bad based on circumstances. How did Peter tie this back into your situation at work?"

"He pointed out three things: One, how we all put labels on events, things, and people. Two, that the label we put on something determines how we choose to react to it. And three, how easy it is for us to perceive something incorrectly because we don't understand the circumstances surrounding it, and then we put a negative label on it. Obviously my relationships at work have deteriorated over the past year because my perceptions of some of the people I work with have somehow changed for the worse."

"So what did he suggest you do?"

"Peter said the first thing we needed to do was to get to the source of the negative perceptions I have. We started by examining each pair of envelopes I had prepared for the various members of the management committee. Peter asked me to identify the specific things each person did that I interpreted as bad. He explained that it was my interpretation of the other person's action that led to my negative view of that person, not the action itself."

"But people do some pretty awful things to other people."

"That's true. But unless you try to understand the reason why the person took the action, you never get a balanced view of that person. He said that no one consciously makes a bad decision."

"What did you do next?"

"We came up with a list of things each person had done that I saw as negative. Then we tried to see if we could change my perspective to see some potential positives in the same action."

"Sounds a little far-fetched to me."

"Actually it worked pretty well. We started off with Lynne. I had described her as negative, problem-oriented, picky, and blunt. Peter saw these as positives."

"What did you put in his coffee?" Karen asked.

Jim chuckled. "He showed me how it was a matter of perspective. Peter encouraged me to really examine Lynne's actions and choose to view them differently. For example, Lynne is always analyzing projects and finding soft spots in them. I originally labelled that as negative and problem-oriented behavior. I could have just as easily described it as realistic and pragmatic. She's a real stickler for details. I labelled her picky when I could have said she was detail-oriented. She openly speaks her mind. I labelled that blunt, when I could have said she is candid. Can you see how my choice of words could make a big difference in how I view her?"

"Hmm . . . I can see how that would make a difference. So after you change the words around, what do you do next?"

"Peter shared some techniques that professional athletes use. We started with some relaxation exercises. Then we practiced visualization and writing affirmations. The objective is to trick your brain into believing that something that hasn't happened yet is a reality."

"Sounds like some of that New Age stuff to me," Karen said with a hint of skepticism in her voice.

"I thought so too, but Peter told me that high-performance professional athletes have been using visualization and relaxation techniques for decades. Controlled experi-

ments have proved that athletes can improve their performance by over 6 percent when they use these two techniques
in combination."

Manion shuffled through some papers in the file folder
next to the bed. "I had to determine the ideal relationship
I'd like to have with each of the management committee
members and picture each of those relationships in my
mind. Then we broke that big picture down into smaller
scenes. Things that had happened recently that didn't go too
well. We practiced running those same situations through
and looking for a different and more positive outcome. Then
we wrote down the end result on these index cards."

He handed Karen a card. "This card is designed to alter
my reaction to Lynne in a typical situation at work where
she makes comments about one of my projects," he said.

Karen studied the card. "But from what you've said to
me, your relationship with her isn't at all like what's described here. How is this supposed to change things?"

"It's a form of preprogramming. I'm supposed to relax
and visualize the scene that's described on the card. I see
myself in a meeting at work, and Lynne has just made a
comment or suggestion about one of my projects. Rather
than jump down her throat or get defensive, I picture myself
being genuinely interested in her opinion and asking her an
open-ended question to find out more about her suggestion,
all the while maintaining my composure. That way I focus
on the reaction I want to have, not the one I would currently
have."

Karen studied the reverse side of the card. "How do you
use this sentence?"

"The other side of the card has a structured statement,
an affirmation, I've written to reinforce the mental imagery
we were just talking about. Having a consistent picture and
an affirming statement really cements the new behavior in
my mind. When one of these situations comes up in real

life, my mind will be preprogrammed to automatically de-
fault to the new behavior. It's creating a new habit through
mental rehearsal."

Focus on the reactions you want to have, not the ones you currently have.

"So how long is it supposed to take for this new pro-
gramming to work?" asked Karen.

"If I'm really diligent about doing my exercises, Peter
said I should start to see tangible differences within the next
month or so."

"How often do you have to practice?"

"Well, I'm going to work on three or four specific behaviors to start with. Peter said I should practice about five
times a day."

"When are you going to find the time?"

"It only takes about four or five minutes for each session. The relaxation part is a form of controlled breathing
exercise, similar to the Lamaze training you went through
in the prenatal classes. That takes about a minute or two.
Reviewing the affirmation statement and doing the visualization takes less than a minute for each scene. If you run
through the exercise five times a day, you're only talking
about twenty to thirty minutes in total. The way I figure it,
if I'm not willing to commit a half hour every day to save
my career, maybe they should fire me."

"A half hour spread throughout the day doesn't seem
too bad. Just using the relaxation technique four or five
times during the day should help you feel more refreshed,"
Karen commented.

"Sure, that would be the minimum benefit I would get

from the exercises. The potential of getting myself back on track is what really excites me," said Manion.

Jim handed his wife the stainless-steel bolt Miller had given him. "Peter gave me a bizarre gift yesterday."

"What's it for?" Karen asked as she examined the four-inch bolt.

"Peter told me to keep it visible around the office and at home. He said it was to remind me of the path we're all on. I thought it was a little strange, and then I remembered the photograph behind his desk in his office. I'd never paid much attention to it before. It's a framed picture of a bolt like this one," explained Manion.

"So what does this bolt of Miller's mean?" she asked.

"Peter wouldn't give me all the details. . . . He said I wasn't ready yet. He did explain that the bolt represents our personal performance. See how the thread is cut?"

"Uh-huh."

"Miller calls it the performance spiral. As he puts it, the quality of our work, our performance, is never static. We're either getting a little better and going up the threads on the bolt, or we're getting a little worse and spiralling down the threads of the bolt. Obviously the past year I somehow got on the downward spiral at work. In my case, the first stage in getting myself going up again is to get in touch with my perceptions and accept responsibility for the relationships my perceptions create."

■

The first stage in getting yourself on the upward spiral is to get in touch with your perceptions and accept responsibility for the relationships your perceptions create.

■

Karen handed the bolt back to her husband. "I'm just happy to see you with some energy and focus again. Do you still have a meeting next week with Philippe Fontaine?"

"Tuesday morning."

"How do you think it'll go?"

Jim held up Miller's bolt and an index card. "I'm working on a positive outcome."

8

It was only ten minutes to eight on Monday morning when Lynne Donato's telephone started to ring. She had come in early to go over the plant expansion feasibility study she had commissioned in the fall. She glanced at the clock on her desk thinking, "Either someone is on the ball or on a spin cycle this morning." She answered the phone.

"Hey Lynne, good morning! Thought I saw your car out in the parking lot. Are you trying to make some brownie points by coming in early?"

She recognized the voice immediately. "Good morning, Ted."

Ted Wilkinson was the company's national sales manager. He had been with the firm almost fourteen years, just three months longer than Lynne. Both had been recruited straight off campus and had worked themselves up to management ranks.

"How's your schedule this morning?" he asked Lynne.

"I'm a little tight. Actually I was just starting to go over the new plant feasibility study when you called. What's up?"

"Well, if you can spare ten minutes, I thought I would bop over and bring you a coffee. Cream and sugar, right?"

"This wouldn't be Ted with the Trojan coffee, would it?"

Wilkinson chuckled. "Aw, come on Lynne. I only need ten minutes of your time. Are all you grads from eastern schools always so stingy with your fellow workers?"

"OK Ted, ten minutes. Then I'm going to toss your butt out of here."

"Great, I'll be over as soon as I pour you your morning dose of caffeine."

Lynne cracked a slight smile and shook her head as she put the receiver down. "I wonder what he's up to this morning?" she thought. "You never know with Ted."

A few minutes later there was a light knock on her office door. The door opened slightly and Ted peeked in.

"Does my ten minutes start from when I greet you or from when I put your coffee on your desk?"

"If I had any sense it would have started nine minutes ago" was Lynne's reply.

"Oh, a little testy this morning, are we? Maybe this extra shot of caffeine will put you over the top. Not to worry, I've taken CPR."

Ted walked into Lynne's office and placed two coffees on her desk then turned around and closed her office door. "Did you hear the scuttlebutt going around late last week?"

Lynne picked up her coffee and sipped it slowly, eyeing Wilkinson. "No, I haven't heard a word."

"You're just playing cute with me. You must have heard about Manion."

Donato was genuinely taken aback. Closed doors with Wilkinson usually meant that he had some especially juicy gossip or that he was fishing for information. Whenever there was the slightest bit of gossip in the office, Wilkinson was bound to hear about it. But Lynne also knew that Ted's sources were pretty reliable.

"Really Ted, I haven't heard anything about Jim."

"Rumor has it he's on the way out."

"Wilkinson, where do you get such wild ideas? Manion's done some great work for us. That product launch a few years ago was the biggest in the company's history."

"The winds are changing in the corporate jungle. It's not what you did for the company a couple of years ago that counts. It's what you did today. Think about it, what's Manion done lately?"

> *It's not what you did for the company a couple of years ago that counts. It's what you did today.*

Lynne chose to ignore Ted's last comment and paused long enough to force him to continue talking.

"There hasn't been anything new coming out of marketing for nearly a year. And you know how difficult it's been working with Manion lately. I seem to remember you locking horns with him a couple of times over the past year."

"Jim and I have had our differences of opinion."

"Come on, Lynne, they were much more than that."

"OK Ted, I'll agree that Manion's been pretty pigheaded on a couple of occasions as far as manufacturing's concerned, and he hasn't been as open to input as he used to be. But remember, Jim and I got along very well in the past. Any disagreements we've had have been about business. It's never been anything personal. What makes you think he's in trouble anyway?"

"Remember last week's management committee meeting?"

"Yeah, we finally got our budgets put together."

"Manion's budget got skewered pretty good. Fisher took

him out to lunch afterward. Rumor has it she read him the riot act."

"Having lunch with the president hardly constitutes a corporate death sentence, Ted."

"Believe what you want. I know he didn't come back after lunch. When Fisher got back she called Fontaine for a closed-door session. How many of those has she had over the past seven years?"

"You've been watching too many courtroom dramas on television, Ted. Listen to yourself. . . . You're making mountains out of circumstantial molehills."

"Did you see or hear from Manion on Friday? No. You know why? He stayed in his office the whole day with his nose buried in his files."

"We'd all probably perform better with a little more disciplined approach."

"I think he's been told to straighten out. Manion only hides in his office like that when he's stressed out. There's no urgent projects going on in marketing. Where else would the stress be coming from? I figure he's under the corporate magnifying glass."

Donato tried to brush off Wilkinson's comments with a halfhearted chuckle. "Remind me not to be caught with my nose to the grindstone for too long. Next you'll be predicting things about me."

Ted crossed his arms over his chest and looked at Lynne. "I'll tell you one thing. If Manion has a closed door with Fontaine this week, you can put money on it; there's a target on his back."

"The company has never operated like that in the past. People get a fair chance to turn themselves around. There have been a few people who've hit rough stretches. They were given time to work things out," Lynne shot back.

Ted's lips drew tight, and his gaze narrowed. "Lynne, it may look circumstantial to you, but from where I sit the evidence is pretty overwhelming. Manion's on the way out. Face it, Lynne, how good does marketing have to be when your people are producing high-quality products and my field staff are hustling their buns peddling the stuff?"

"Ted, let's not forget that it was Jim who came up with the market research and analysis that led to our last big product introduction. That product line now produces over 20 percent of our net profits. Manion developed the concept, the segmentation, and the positioning."

"A lot of people figure he was in the right place at the right time," Ted replied.

"There's more to it than simply timing. He's got a good, creative mind as well as sharp analytical skills." Lynne struggled to stay calm and factual. "I'd be the first to admit that Jim hasn't been the easiest guy to work with the past six months. And, yes, I've had a couple of run-ins with him. Maybe he's got some personal problems he's sorting out. All I know is he's done a lot of good things for the company. You've seen the ROI tracking system he developed for our marketing programs. Nobody in our industry has got anything even remotely close to it. Our market share is up dramatically. . . . I can't imagine the powers that be even thinking about giving up on him."

Wilkinson got up from his chair. "Well, I'm not from the Pollyanna school of management, Donato. The signs are pretty clear to me that Manion's going to be toast. What do you think will happen after he's gone?"

"There's no way I'm going to speculate about anything like that," she replied.

"That's your choice. I figure there might be some structural changes coming. Maybe some departments will merge." Wilkinson looked at his watch. "I'd better be going before my butt gets imprinted with your footprint. Catch you later."

Donato went back to examining the feasibility study for

the proposed expansion but found she was unable to focus her attention on it. She kept thinking about Manion. Finally she got up and put on her coat. Suddenly she needed some fresh air.

9

MANION ARRIVED AT THE OFFICE BEFORE SEVEN-THIRTY on Tuesday morning. He closed his door and went through his breathing and visualization exercises a number of times to prepare for his meeting with Philippe Fontaine.

"I wonder if I can catch Philippe early this morning before most of the staff gets in?" he thought. "Maybe I can arrange to meet him off-site."

Ever since his luncheon with Katherine Fisher, Jim had felt like a marked man whenever he was in the office complex. Yesterday it had been difficult to keep his thoughts under control. He was beginning to feel paranoid, second-guessing casual comments from other staff members and worrying that his personal credibility would be lost if news of his meeting with Katherine became public.

Since his session with Peter Miller on Saturday, Jim had used the breathing exercise whenever he felt his tension level rising. He was particularly tense this morning. The breathing didn't seem to be working. Manion picked up the telephone and called Miller's office.

"Peter, I was hoping I'd catch you this morning."

"Morning Jim. Something wrong? You sound like you're wound tighter than a spring."

"I feel really tight. I've been trying to use the breathing exercise you gave me, but it doesn't seem to be working. I guess this meeting with Fontaine has got me really keyed up."

"We'll just dip into our bag of tricks. Let me give you a visualization you can use along with the breathing. It should help calm you down," said Peter.

"You must have read my mind. That's exactly what I was hoping you would be able to do," replied Manion.

"I'd like you to think about a thermometer. The kind with a big red bulb at the bottom. Picture the bulb of the thermometer sitting right inside your stomach and the shaft of the thermometer running up through your chest to your neck and then into your head. The highest temperature rating is in your brain. Have you got the picture?" Miller asked.

"OK, I've got it pretty clear."

"Now try to get a sense of the stress level in your body and visualize it as a temperature reading on the thermometer. Next, while you're doing your breathing exercise, I want you to visualize the level of the mercury in the shaft of the thermometer slowly coming down. Keep concentrating on the mercury coming down until it's all in the bulb. If you do it right, you should feel a warm sensation in your stomach and upper abdomen."

"Thanks Peter. It seems easy enough. I'll work on it more, as soon as I'm off the phone," replied Jim.

"What time is your meeting with Fontaine?" Miller asked.

"It's supposed to be at ten. I'm going to see if I can get to him early. I hope I can get him to agree to an off-site meeting. I think I'd feel a lot more comfortable talking to him if we were out of the office. Maybe I'm just getting paranoid."

"It's a good idea to find some neutral ground. I'm sure

Fontaine will be feeling some stress over the meeting as well. This situation brings back a lot of memories from my days as an outplacement specialist. I don't think I'll ever get over the look in people's faces when they got bad news from me."

"I don't think that will be the point of the meeting today. Katherine gave me strong indications we weren't past the point of no return. Philippe probably wants to assess where my head is at."

"And where is it?"

"I think I'm OK. I know I'm feeling really stressed about the meeting, but I don't think I'm afraid. I just want to get it over with and move on to the next stage, whatever that may be."

"How's the picture of the meeting playing in your mind? Have you been running through various scenarios?" Miller asked.

"Yes. I've been running through all kinds of variations of the meeting in my head. You were right, when you practice all the potential scenes you're able to start to predict which ones will play out in a positive way."

"That's right, Jim. It's important to keep in mind that a conversation is like going downstream in a canoe. As long as you know where the rocks are, the ride can be pretty smooth. Lose your concentration and you'll likely capsize. By rehearsing the scenes mentally you'll be better able to identify and avoid the triggers that might move the meeting in the wrong direction. I'm just doing paperwork this morning, so if you need anything else, just pick up the phone."

"Thanks Peter, I'll give you a call a little later and let you know how the meeting went."

After Manion hung up the telephone he began to practice the thermometer visualization. He could feel the tension in the back of his neck and shoulders subsiding. He turned on his computer and sent Fontaine an e-mail message asking him to call as soon as he got in. Then he took out a few project files to work on. About twenty minutes later the telephone rang.

"Good morning, Jim. It's Philippe. I got your e-mail. What's up?"

"Thanks for calling, Philippe. I was wondering how you felt about going out of the office for our meeting today. I'd probably be a little more comfortable. Do you mind?"

"No, I don't mind at all. Is ten o'clock still good for you? My schedule has cleared up a little bit, so we could get together earlier if you wanted to."

"I'd rather get to it earlier than later."

"What's your morning like?"

"You were going to be my first scheduled appointment today."

"Why don't we slip out to a restaurant and grab a bite to eat or something. Do you want to drive or should I?"

"I'd be more comfortable if we took separate cars and met at the restaurant. You can pick the place."

"OK, how about that small diner at the corner of Grant and Fifth?"

"Sounds good. What time?" asked Jim.

"How about a quarter to nine. I don't have anything else planned until after lunch. That way we can spend a couple of hours if we need to," Fontaine said.

Manion looked at his watch as he hung up the telephone. "It's almost eight. Philippe will probably leave about eight-thirty," he thought. "I'll leave now so that it won't be so obvious that we're meeting. I'll write a note for Amy saying I've got an appointment at the advertising agency."

Jim slipped on his overcoat and grabbed his briefcase as well as his large portfolio case to lend credibility to his story. He jotted down a quick note to Amy and dropped it off at the switchboard as he left.

Manion took the route along the river to get to Grant Street. He stopped for a few minutes in a small park to enjoy the scenery and collect his thoughts. The park was empty, but he could swear he heard the sounds of children playing and laughing. Memories of Bryan and Jennifer filled his mind. He looked at a swing set and saw Karen pushing the children on the swings. He heard them squealing with delight. He could see Karen's face, the smile that was always there for him. He remembered the softness of her skin as they walked hand in hand along the riverbank. It was then that Jim realized his tension had vanished.

Manion arrived at the diner first and picked a small table against the back wall. "It's like being a gunslinger in the Old West," he thought. "Always face the door and keep your back against the wall."

Within a few minutes Philippe Fontaine arrived and greeted Jim warmly. "Thanks for taking the time to meet with me, Jim. I really appreciate it. I know how busy things are at the office."

The men scanned the menu briefly and placed their orders. "Jim, I'm not the type to pussyfoot around. You know that Katherine has some concerns. I'm sure you have some too. What I'd like us to do is put our cards on the table and discuss this situation in a calm and rational manner," said Fontaine.

"Philippe, I appreciate your giving me some time to think after my meeting with Katherine last week. To be perfectly honest, I doubt if I could have handled this very professionally last week," replied Manion.

"Thanks for your candor, Jim. If you're in agreement, I'd like to summarize our concerns just to make sure that we all have a clear understanding. Then I'd like us to spend most of our time discussing what we can do to put the situation back on track. Is that OK with you?"

"That's fine, Philippe. Maybe you could start with the summary."

The two men chatted until almost twenty after nine. Fontaine was very clear and nonjudgmental in his descriptions of Manion's behavior. For his part, Jim asked numerous questions, sought clarification on a couple of key issues, and made notes on a pad.

"Jim, Katherine respects the work you've done and the contributions you've made to the company. If you're waiting for a letter to document this meeting, you'll be waiting a long time. There isn't going to be one. There's not going to be any formal documentation in your file. Katherine specifically doesn't want to do that. Even though there won't be a paper trail, I think you realize that we do have a serious situation to deal with."

"I appreciate that, Philippe. Katherine made it clear last week as well."

"It's serious but not insurmountable. We do have a pretty tight time frame."

"How tight?"

"We'd like to see noticeable changes within three months."

"And if not . . . I assume there will be a package."

Fontaine was a little surprised by Manion's directness. "Yes Jim, there would be a package. One that would be more than equitable."

Manion's gaze locked onto Philippe's. "That's what I expected, Philippe." Jim's voice lowered. "I've been thinking a lot about the past year. I haven't been the easiest person to work with . . . no excuses. But . . . I don't want a package. I don't want to leave. I want to make the changes needed and put this behind me."

Manion paused to collect his thoughts. "Philippe, I need to know specifically what you want me to do. I need you to paint me a clear picture of the changes you expect to see three months down the road. I also want to know what support I can expect from you and the company."

◾
---

*P*aint a clear picture of the changes you
expect to see.

◾

"Without question we're going to have to see improvement with your relationships with other members of the management team. That means the elimination of the aggressiveness and defensiveness you've been showing, especially in meetings. You'll also need to be more open-minded when suggestions are tabled."

"And what help can I expect from you?"

"If you agree, I'd like to meet with you once a week to review your performance. If I see anything that needs more immediate comment, I'll make sure to bring it to your attention, discreetly of course. I'll act as an extra set of eyes to help you gauge your progress. The company's going to give you a fair chance to turn this around." Philippe put his hand on Manion's shoulder. "And I'll be here for you as a sounding board. You're not in this alone, Jim."

10

Manion dropped another quarter in the slot on the pay phone and called the office. "Hello Amy, this is Jim. I got tied up a little longer than anticipated at my agency meeting this morning. I'm going to stop for lunch on my way back to the office. If anyone's looking for me, I should be back by about one-thirty. Thanks."

Jim hung up the phone and headed to his car. He was going to meet with Peter Miller. Along the way he dropped into a delicatessen and picked up some sandwiches and sodas. Within ten minutes he was at Miller's office.

Peter looked up from his desk as Manion entered. "It's about time. I'm starved. What did you bring for munchies?"

"Your choice of pastrami, ham and cheese, smoked turkey, or roast beef . . . and a few sodas."

"Ham and cheese and a ginger ale sounds great. How did your meeting with Fontaine go this morning?"

"As well as could be expected. Philippe seems to really want to help me get turned around. We had a long chat about the company's concerns about my attitude and my ability to work with the other members of the senior team. I made some notes on the conversation." Jim handed his pad to Miller.

Peter studied the notes for a few minutes then quipped, "You should have pursued a career in medicine. Your handwriting is bad enough! Well . . . there's enough here for us to work on, that's for sure. How much time have they given you?"

"They expect to see noticeable improvement within three months."

Miller opened his sandwich. "In that case we'll have to decide which issues are going to be the most visible and easiest to fix within that time frame. What departments do you interact with the most?"

"Probably production and sales."

"Who heads up those departments?"

"Lynne Donato for production and Ted Wilkinson for sales."

Miller looked at Jim and snapped open his can of ginger ale. "I seem to recall that on Saturday we classified your relationship with those two as . . . strained. Maybe I'm being too kind."

"Yeah, they've been quite a challenge lately."

Miller shook his head. "You're not making this any easier for yourself. Did you get along better with them in the past?"

"My relationship with Lynne was excellent for a long time. It seems to have been strained during the past year. Ted's always been difficult."

"Well, out of the seven committee members they're the two you're going to have to really key in on." Peter reviewed Manion's notes more thoroughly as he ate his sandwich and sipped on the soda. "You must have meetings coming up and some new projects in the pipeline."

"Sure. We have a regular management committee meeting every second Monday. I'm working on a number of new product proposals. I'll have plenty of opportunity to work with Ted and Lynne over the next few months."

"Good, but let's not get too far ahead of ourselves. Give

me more details on your talk with Fontaine. What did you commit to do, and how is he going to help you?"

Peter listened intently as Manion gave him a detailed account of the conversation. Occasionally Miller jotted down a few brief notes. Peter watched his friend's body language and gestures and listened to the tone and speed of his voice. Within ten minutes Manion had finished describing his meeting with Philippe.

"Is that one pastrami?" Miller asked. "Good, I'll take it." Peter opened up the wrapping on the sandwich as he spoke. "Jim, you realize that it will take significant effort to turn this situation around. Somehow you're going to have to get other members of the management committee on your side within the three-month window if you expect to pull this off. If Fontaine comes through with the ongoing coaching and regular meetings he's promised, that will be a big help. From what you've said about him, he must be pretty influential."

Manion, his mouth full, nodded.

Peter continued, "You're at the end of the diving board, and it's time to jump into the pool. I think it's time for an advanced swimming lesson."

Miller turned his chair so he was at a ninety-degree angle to the wall behind his desk. "Only you can turn your life around." He pointed at the photograph of the stainless-steel bolt. "It's time we got into some detail about my friend here and how you can use him."

Manion looked at the photograph. "The performance spiral."

Peter flipped to a fresh piece of paper on Manion's notepad. "I can't think without a pen in my hand. Let me draw the process. To start with, let's think of it as a circle. You remember where the process starts."

"Sure," said Manion. "It starts with my perceptions of the world around me. The people I work with. Myself. The company. Customers. My family. Everything."

"Right, and it's your perceptions that determine the kinds of relationships you're going to create with those people. If you have a positive perspective toward someone, you'll create a positive relationship. If the freeze-frame is stuck on something negative, you'll create a negative relationship. Remember, once your mind has labelled someone or something, it tries to prove it was right."

"That's why we worked on learning how to separate what people do from how we interpret what they do. The action itself is simply an event. It's how I process that event that makes it good or bad in my mind," said Manion.

■

What people do is simply an event. How you process that event makes it good or bad.

■

"Absolutely," said Peter. "We already worked through your envelopes. We identified the actions that you originally saw as negative for each person on the management committee. Then we tried to change your frame of reference so you could see the positives in those same actions. Lynne was a classic case."

Peter drew a circle on the notepad with his pen then divided the circle into eight sections. He labelled the first section PERCEPTIONS and the second one RELATIONSHIPS.

Miller opened his left-hand desk drawer and pulled out two magnets. "I always use these to reinforce the first two stages of the performance spiral." He handed the magnets to Jim.

"What happens when you roll the magnets around in the palm of your hand?" he asked Manion.

"They eventually get lined up where they attract each other, and they link up," he answered.

"That's the natural inclination of human beings. We're pack animals. We want to form structured groups. We want to form relationships. Nature didn't design us as solitary hunters. If we could get rid of the external pressures society forces on us in terms of success, possessions, and the like, people would be more likely to act like these two magnets. Unfortunately, we can't transform society overnight and rid ourselves of the negative conditioning that permeates our culture. What happens to the magnets when they aren't aligned correctly and you try to force them together?"

"They push away from each other."

"Can you exert enough force to make them connect when they're in that position?"

"No, I can't push them together hard enough."

"That's what happens when you try to force a relationship where negative perceptions exist. You can try as hard as you want, but it's not going to work. What's the only way you can get the two magnets together?"

"I have to turn one of them around."

"Jim, keep that thought foremost in your mind every day for the next few months. It's absolutely critical that you take responsibility for turning your perceptions around, as if you were one of the magnets. Your success is totally dependent on it." Miller put out his hand, "Let me show you something else these magnets can teach us."

If you want to improve the relationships in your life, you must take responsibility by altering your perceptions.

Manion handed Peter the magnets. Peter placed one magnet on the top of Jim's notepad and held the other underneath the pad. "This is a little illustration of teamwork. Remember when you were a kid and you would pretend you were doing magic tricks by using magnetic force to move a metal object?"

"I was the Great Manini in grade four," Manion said with a smile.

"In this illustration your notepad is an obstacle. When I get the two magnets properly aligned on either side of the pad, see how they move in unison? Their attraction, their commitment to each other, goes through the obstacle. They can function as a team. They can communicate even through adversity. If there is one lesson I wish I could teach every CEO in the country, it is the importance of building positive relationships in the workplace. Strong personal relationships throughout a company are essential to creating an interdependent environment. They foster extraordinary business performance."

Strong personal relationships throughout a company are essential to creating an interdependent environment.

Peter gave the magnets back to Manion. "Why don't you keep these in your office as a reminder."

Jim placed the magnets in his jacket pocket. "Thanks Peter, I will."

Miller flipped back to his diagram of the performance spiral. "Based on what you've told me today, you and Philippe are well along in the process. In fact, you've progressed through the next three stages."

Peter marked the third stage POTENTIAL; the fourth stage OPTIONS; and the fifth one PROJECTS. "The kind of relation-

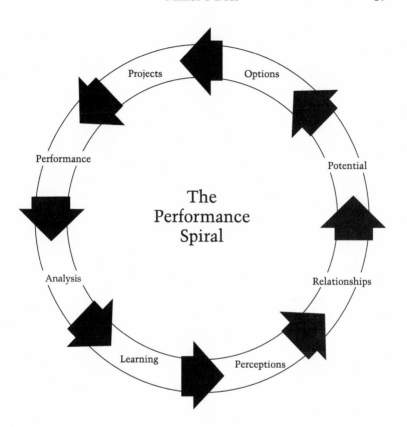

The
Performance
Spiral

Projects

Options

Potential

Performance

Relationships

Analysis

Perceptions

Learning

ship you create with another person determines the relationship's potential. For example, let's say I believe that the
country should close its doors to immigrants because I
think they're all lazy and a drain on our social programs.
With those perceptions I would probably create very poor relationships with any immigrants I might meet. There would
be very little, if any, potential for me to work with them or
become friends. If, on the other hand, I see immigrants as
hardworking and believe that they boost our economy, I

would be more likely to form excellent relationships with them."

"Sure, that makes sense," said Jim.

"So it goes without saying that whenever you have an excellent relationship, you have a lot of potential for the relationship to grow. And the potential of a relationship determines the number and kinds of options you might consider exploring with the other person. For example, you would never go into business with someone you perceived as dishonest. Your relationship wouldn't be strong enough. There would be very little potential in the relationship. Having a business with that person would never even be an option you would consider."

Manion nodded his head in agreement.

"Let's examine your morning with Fontaine, and you'll see how the dynamics of the process work," said Peter. "Based on the first envelope exercise with Philippe as the subject, it's pretty clear you think quite highly of him, your perception of him is positive."

"That's true. And, the second envelope exercise confirmed that the relationship is a positive one," Manion added.

"That strong, positive relationship has a lot of potential. Philippe hasn't given up on you. He is actively working to help you correct the situation. In terms of the performance spiral that's a stage-three type of activity. Stage four is options. You and Philippe discussed a number of things you could do to get back on track. Then you committed to doing certain things to help improve your performance, and he committed to support you. Your weekly review meeting is a good example. That puts the two of you squarely in stage five, the project stage."

"I never really thought of myself as being a project. It sounds so clinical," said Jim.

"Using project management to help yourself is actually

pretty simple. Anytime you have change, you have the opportunity to use project management," Peter explained. "As you know from work, we can look at a project as simply taking an existing state, applying some time and resources to it, and changing it into something else. In that context even getting ready to go to work becomes a project. There's certain things you have to do to get ready—you shower, shave, dress. You use these processes to convert your physical state from sleepy and unkempt to bright-eyed and bushy-tailed. You even allow yourself a prescribed amount of time to accomplish these tasks."

Anytime you have change, you have the opportunity to use project management.

"So in terms of looking at myself as a project, we want to improve upon my current attitudes and behaviors. The specific behavioral changes that Philippe detailed in our meeting this morning—eliminating my aggressiveness and defensiveness, for example—make up the objectives of the project. The due date has been set for three months from now," said Manion.

"And the two of you have assessed what resources you need to dedicate to the project in terms of your mutual time and effort. For a project to be successful, people need to take ownership of their role in it. That's exactly what you and Philippe have done. You've made personal commitments to each other. That brings us to stage six."

"Which is?" asked Jim.

"PERFORMANCE. At the end of the day that's what really matters: did we get the desired result? The performance that you and Philippe generate will be directly proportional to how well you each live up to the commitments you've made to each other. A lot of people in business treat their commitments in a rather cavalier fashion. What they fail to realize is that every time you make a commitment, however small, your personal credibility and image are on the line. A commitment is an intensely personal thing." Miller added the PERFORMANCE label to the diagram.

Every time you make a commitment, however small, your personal credibility and image are on the line.

"So what comes after performance? There are two stages left, aren't there?" asked Manion.

"Funny enough, they're the two most underutilized: ANALYSIS and LEARNING. Once we have carried out the project tasks, we need to measure our performance against the objectives we've set. Regardless of whether we generated better performance than expected or poorer performance than we anticipated, it's critical that we conduct an analysis of the project. Trying to understand why we generated a certain level of performance is the only way we'll continue to grow. Doing the analysis gives us a golden opportunity to learn from our actions, and learning allows us to grow and improve our performance over time."

Trying to understand why we generated a certain level of performance is the only way we'll continue to grow.

"Peter, let's assume that we've done all the stages. What happens then?"

"Well, at that point the circle becomes a spiral. You see, if we follow the process through, we gain new knowledge based on our experiences. Then we have the opportunity to change our perceptions based on the new reality, the knowledge we have discovered," Peter said.

"And then the cycle starts over. . . . Your new perceptions lead to new relationships. Those new relationships define how much potential exists, which then leads to a new or revised set of options to consider. Once we choose an option and make personal commitments to each other, we have another new project. That project generates performance, which we then analyze, gaining new knowledge, which again leads to another new perception, and so on. . . . It sounds incredibly easy," said Manion.

"You're a fast learner, Jim. And you're right, . . . it does sound incredibly easy. The process is very simple. Unfortunately most people fail to follow through."

Miller stood up and pointed to a section of thread on the bolt in the picture. "What would happen if I took a file and scored the threads right here?"

"The nut would jam when it got to that point on the bolt. You'd never get the nut past the damaged area."

"That's what happens with this process. People fail to follow through on all the steps, so their performance gets stuck at a certain level. They get in a rut and tend to blame their work environment, their boss, their coworkers, . . . anyone except themselves. They get bored and start sitting around waiting for someone to stimulate them. Then the illusion sets in," said Peter.

"The illusion?"

"They begin to live with the illusion that their performance is static, in a holding pattern. People fool themselves into thinking they can go on automatic pilot, that they can survive by going through the motions."

---- ▪ ----

We fool ourselves by thinking we can go on automatic pilot, that we can survive by going through the motions.

---- ▪ ----

Jim Manion listened to Miller intently. His stomach felt uneasy, his hands cold.

"Nothing is ever static. The answer is in nature," Peter continued. "Look at any living thing and you'll discover that once the process of growth stops, the process of dying and decay starts. Once people stop learning on the job, their effectiveness slowly starts to erode, and often they become layoff statistics."

"That sounds like a pretty severe prediction, Peter."

"It's more than a prediction. I've witnessed it thousands of times. Continuous improvement isn't just something for the shop floor. It's something we all need to practice regardless of the job we have if we want to keep pace with change and maintain our personal marketability. I've read predictions from futurists that state that half of the jobs in our country today won't even exist in fifteen years. Now that's a wake-up call if ever I heard one!"

"Statistics like that scare the hell out of me, and they must scare a lot of CEOs too. But what can be done?" asked Manion.

"Actually, a lot of the work I'm doing now is helping companies manage change more effectively. We're using the performance spiral model throughout entire organizations. We teach people how to get in touch with their perceptions and use the self-management tools I've been sharing with you so they can get mentally prepared to handle the coming changes. Of course, we also provide practical project management training from the shop floor up. I find that it helps to create a common language and framework within the company." Miller picked up some business magazines from a stack on his desk. "It's amazing to me that with all the change happening in the business environment today so few companies are equipping their people with the skills they need to effectively manage change, personally and professionally."

Manion nodded his head in agreement. "Well, I feel a lot more confident now that you've given me the new techniques—relaxation, visualization, and affirmations. I think my strong project management background will help as well."

Miller looked at his watch. "Hey, if you're going to get back to the office by one-thirty, you'd better hit the road!"

11

"Good morning, Amy. Is Jim Manion in today?" Lynne asked.

"He was in first thing, but he left early for a meeting at the agency. He called and said the meeting was going to take longer than expected. He should be in the office by about one-thirty."

"Would you mind leaving him a note asking him to call me this afternoon?"

"Consider it done, Lynne."

"Thanks Amy."

Donato continued on her way to Katherine Fisher's office to give the president an overview of the plant expansion study.

She knocked on Fisher's door. "I've prepared a summary of the plant expansion study recommendations if you'd like to see them. Do you have a few minutes?"

"Sure, come on in," Katherine answered. "You must have jumped on that report. Didn't it just come in yesterday?"

"I thought we might want to present some of the recommendations at the board meeting. The time line is pretty short if we're going to get slides and handouts ready in time," replied Lynne.

"Good point. Let's go over to the conference table and see what you've got."

Donato arrived at the table first and picked the chair facing the door in Katherine's office. After Fisher was seated, Donato handed her a copy of the summary of the recommendations and walked the president through each of the recommendations, answering Fisher's additional questions as they went along.

"Lynne, this is very well prepared. I think we should present this summary and some relevant details at the board meeting. Prepare some supplemental printed material that the board members can take away with them. I'd like to have you make the presentation. Plan for a maximum of fifteen minutes for presenting the material, and maybe another fifteen for questions from the board. Jim's department is coordinating the production of all the slides and printed material for the meeting, so check on deadlines with them."

"I'll speak to Jim later this afternoon."

"This plant expansion is going to cost us more than we expected. The board may give us a bit of a rough time with it, especially with sales being a little soft lately. Wilkinson and Manion will be in the hot seat. They'll have to explain where we're going to get the additional revenues to pay for the expansion."

"Virtually all of the current drop-off can be attributed to the seasonal cycle of a couple of our major markets," Donato observed. "Even so, we're running at over 78 percent. When the market comes back we'll face the same supply shortages we did last summer and fall. Not having enough capacity will hurt our bottom line."

"Maybe so . . . I'm just anticipating that the board may feel we haven't been as aggressive as we could have been over the past year. The last major product launch two years ago really solidified a couple of new markets for us. We've just been twiddling our thumbs since then," Katherine ventured.

Fisher glanced at her watch as she pushed her chair away from the conference table. "Have you ever noticed how quickly time goes when there's a board meeting looming on the horizon?"

Donato gathered her material. "A little external motivation does us all a little good from time to time."

"Anything else?" Fisher asked.

Lynne cast a nervous glance toward the door then looked at Katherine and studied her for a few seconds. "No. . . . I'd better get started on getting this presentation put together."

Files in hand, Donato left Fisher's office. Katherine watched her leave, sensing something wasn't quite right. She went to her desk and dialed Philippe's number. "You're back. . . . How did your first meeting with Manion go this morning?"

"I think there are a few things we should discuss."

"Anything urgent?"

"Not necessarily urgent, but I'd like to tend to them today while they're still fresh in my mind. I don't need much of your time. Maybe half an hour," replied Fontaine.

"Now's a good time. Most of the staff is out for lunch, so it's pretty quiet."

Philippe arrived within a couple of minutes, closing the door to Katherine's office as he entered. "I spent quite a bit of time with Jim this morning. There are a few things I want to go over with you."

Fisher motioned for Fontaine to sit at the conference table. "How did he take the lunch meeting I had with him last week?"

"He admitted that it was a good thing he had some time to cool off before I got to see him."

"Was he pretty hot?"

"Not so much hot as shocked, . . . surprised, . . . hurt. He really didn't have a clue there was a problem," Philippe said. "Considering the circumstances, he was a lot calmer than I expected."

"That's good."

"Actually I was pretty impressed with his approach to the situation. He'd obviously done a lot of thinking about it. He'd even gone so far as to solicit some outside counsel."

"Legal?" Katherine's eyebrows drew down and her gaze narrowed.

"No, not at all. He's seeing a performance enhancement specialist."

"He's done all that since we had lunch last Wednesday?"

"Yes, he's already had a couple of meetings, and he's actively working on a program for self-improvement."

"I didn't expect that at all, especially at this stage."

"Neither did I. Katherine, your meeting really shook Manion up. He seems to be very sincere in his desire to correct the situation and get back on track with the company."

"Well, that's as much as we could have hoped for at this stage." Katherine's face relaxed momentarily. "The big question is whether he'll be able to actually pull off a personal turnaround. I'm not sure whether he's passed the point of no return with the other staff members. That will be the litmus test."

"I think he realizes he has a lot of bridges to mend and it's going to take some time to get that accomplished."

"Philippe, it's one thing to say that he realizes what he needs to do. It's another for him to actually do it. The bottom line is we've got a plant expansion on the drawing board, and sales have softened up. The board may be concerned that we haven't introduced any new products for over a year. Our marketing programs are the same ones they saw last meeting. I'm a little worried they'll think we've been sitting on our rumps."

"Katherine, let's remember that the five-year plan didn't call for any new product introductions until this coming fall. The new products we introduced two years ago took more of our plant capacity than we thought they would. Until we get the expansion approved and completed, we really don't have the capacity to handle a new line anyway."

"Assuming our sales increase."

"We've gone through this softening every year for the past eight or nine years. I don't see any reason why things won't rebound like they have in the past," Fontaine said.

Fisher crossed her arms and leaned away from the table. "That's the second time I've heard that this morning. I hope you're right."

Fontaine casually opened one of the file folders he had brought with him and took out a pad of writing paper. "You seem a little tense lately, Katherine. Anything on your mind?"

Fisher scanned the walls of her office before answering Philippe. "I don't know, maybe it's just me. I've been feeling a little edgy lately. Maybe it's the board meeting. Maybe it's the numbers."

"Maybe it's Jim Manion?" asked Fontaine.

Katherine's head lowered. She raised her hand and pinched the bridge of her nose. "Yes, maybe it's Jim Manion. I guess I haven't been able to deal with the mixed emotions I've been having about this situation. Part of me knows we have to get him straightened out and functioning better with the other members of the team. I really want him to come around. He's been an integral part of our success since he joined us. But then I realize that if he can't or won't come around, I'll need to get rid of him. It's a tough decision."

"Anything else?"

Katherine sat motionless looking at Philippe. Then she got up and went to the window in her office. She stared out in silence. After a few minutes she said, "I guess I have this sense of personal failure. When you hire someone and watch them succeed, it's really a gut-wrenching experience to then have to witness them self-destruct."

She turned to face Philippe. "But the bottom line is that it doesn't really matter what you think of someone on a personal basis. You have to live with the fact that you're paid to do what's best for the company."

Fontaine responded, "I think it's called the burden of office."

Katherine looked out the window again. "Yeah, the burden of office." She stood silently for a few seconds then asked Fontaine, "Have you noticed anything with Lynne Donato lately? She was in to see me earlier today, and I couldn't help feeling there was something on her mind. For some reason she just didn't feel comfortable talking. It was very strange."

"No, I haven't noticed anything unusual. I'll make a point of dropping by her office this afternoon or tomorrow morning. We have a good relationship. Maybe she'll feel comfortable enough to open up with me."

"Thanks, I'd really appreciate your taking the time to do that, Philippe."

"Katherine, can we get back to one of the comments you made a few moments ago?"

"Sure."

"When you were talking about Jim Manion, you said you felt a sense of personal failure. Usually when people feel that way it's because they feel responsible in some way. Is that how you feel?"

"I suppose so. I'm second-guessing myself. Maybe I feel I haven't done everything I could have done. Remember last week when you asked me whether my reactions to Jim had changed? At the time I totally ruled out that possibility. If I'm honest with myself I have to admit I'm not sure."

"Katherine, there's something the performance enhancement specialist did with Jim that I think may be of value for us as well," said Fontaine.

"Manion gave you details of the program he's working on?"

"During our meeting this morning we got into a discussion about the overall process he's working through. Jim described a couple of exercises I hadn't come across before, so I asked him to elaborate. If you have a little bit more time right now, we could do the two exercises. I think they could really help us deal with the situation."

Fisher came back to the conference table and sat down next to Fontaine. "OK, Philippe, what do I have to do?"

Fontaine handed her a pen and two sheets of blank paper. "On the first sheet of paper I want you to write down anything that comes to mind when I ask you to describe Jim Manion. We won't spend much time on it, maybe two or three minutes, so just jot down your thoughts as quickly as possible. After you've finished that we'll start on the second exercise."

Katherine took the top off her pen, thought for a moment, then started writing.

12

"Hello Lynne, it's Jim. Amy said you wanted me to call you as soon as I got in from my agency meeting."

"Thanks for getting back to me. There are a few things I'd like to talk to you about. I'd like to drop by your office and see you this afternoon if you have the time."

Manion flipped through his appointment calendar. "I've got a media rep coming in at three. That shouldn't take more than about twenty minutes. Other than that I can work around your schedule."

"How about two o'clock?"

"Fine. Do I need to get anything ready for you?"

"No, I need to put together some presentation material for the board meeting. I suppose you want me to have everything typed up and coded to layouts for you, just like with the last presentation."

Manion remembered the heated words he and Lynne had exchanged over the last presentation and was determined not to repeat the scene. "Do you have some summary text?"

"What do you need that for if I give you typed copy and layouts?" asked Lynne, sounding a bit impatient.

"Well, I thought we could use your summary text as

long as you underlined the specific parts you want to use. That would save you some time, wouldn't it?"

"Sure, but I don't need hassles with changes later on. There's not much time until the board meeting."

Jim was well aware of the deadlines and was having a hard time keeping his cool. "Lynne, I'm sure we'll be able to do a good job working from your summary notes. Let's give it a try."

"OK, see you at two, Jim."

Donato hung up the telephone and grabbed the summary she had prepared for Katherine Fisher. After making an additional copy, she returned to her office and started to highlight her key presentation points. Within twenty minutes she had finished. Then she jotted down some notes to remind her about the other items she wanted to discuss with Manion. At two o'clock she put her telephone on call forward and headed for Jim's office.

"Amy, I'll be in with Jim Manion for about the next hour," Donato said as she passed the receptionist. "We're working on some presentation material for the board meeting, so I'd rather not be disturbed unless it's a matter of life and death."

Donato hurried past the row of offices on her way to visit with Manion. She tapped on his door. "Are you still OK for time Jim?"

"Sure, why don't you come in and close the door so we won't get interrupted." Manion dialed the extension of one of his staff members. "Carole, can you come over and help Lynne and me put her board presentation together? Good, just tap on my door and come in."

Jim looked at Donato and continued, "Carole will be here in just a minute. She's looking after all the production for the board meeting and has a good handle on deadlines, format and so on."

"Good, things are pretty hectic around here with the

board meeting coming up, and we don't have time for a second chance."

Jim was struggling to hold his tongue when Carole knocked on his door and walked in. Manion suggested that all three of them cluster around his conference table to go over Donato's material. "Lynne, why don't you walk us through your presentation so we can key the order. Carole, if you need any clarification on what's needed, be sure to ask. We don't have much time to get this material together, and there's virtually no time for remakes."

The three of them went over Donato's sheets in detail and wrapped their discussion up by two-forty-five. Manion turned to Carole. "Thanks. You've made some excellent suggestions. Can you give Lynne a call in the morning and let her know when the studio will have the first drafts ready for proofing?"

As Carole left his office, Jim turned to Lynne. "You mentioned there were a few other things we needed to get done this afternoon. What else do you have?"

"I'm not sure how interested you'll be in the first one. I got a call from the community college where I sit on the industry advisory board. Anyway, they called yesterday afternoon and asked if someone here might be available to be a guest lecturer for their advanced marketing class. They're wrapping up the section on communications, and they thought a real-life industry perspective would be important for the students. I thought you might be interested in helping the students."

"Yeah, I suppose I could. Did they give you any details about what they're looking for and when?"

"It would be an afternoon session, about two hours. They want you to talk about how you design a communication program right from ground zero. Objectives, media selection, creative development, measurement criteria . . . the whole thing. They don't need you to show any creative concepts. It's really a focus on the management side of communications."

"When would they want me to do the session?"

"Three weeks from this coming Thursday." Donato looked at the calendar on Jim's wall. "That would make it Thursday the fourteenth."

"What time?"

"From one to three in the afternoon."

"At the main campus?"

"Uh-huh, lecture hall A. I can get you a map of the campus."

"Why, afraid I'll get lost?" Manion winced as his sarcasm slipped out.

"No, I'm just trying to be helpful."

He bit his lower lip as he looked at Lynne. "Hey, it actually sounds like it could be fun. It's been quite a while since I've done a presentation in an academic environment. Who do I follow up with to finalize things?"

Lynne peeled a sheet off her notepad. "Here's the name and number of the contact."

Manion took the sheet from Lynne. "I'll call them after my next appointment."

"Thanks, Jim. I'm sure your presentation will put things in perspective for the students." Lynne paused then continued nervously, "The last thing I wanted to discuss briefly was the board meeting. You know we're going to present our plant expansion plans."

"That's evident from the visuals we're making for you."

"Well, Katherine's a little concerned about our decline in sales during the past few months. She thinks it might be a sticky point with the board," said Lynne.

Manion studied her for a few moments. "It's no big deal. . . . We have a seasonal downturn every year at this time."

"I mentioned that to her," Donato hesitated, not sure how she should continue.

Manion leaned forward in his chair. "You mentioned that to her, and . . . "

"Well, she didn't seem to accept the fact too readily. She seems to think we haven't been as aggressive as we should have been over the past year. I don't know, maybe she's feeling a bit more stress than usual. She seems to be pretty uptight."

Jim paused to collect his thoughts. "Well, there's been a lot going on around here lately. It's probably nothing to worry about. I can take it up with Katherine later. Thanks for letting me know, Lynne. It will help me plan my presentation strategy for the board meeting."

Donato looked at her watch. "It's ten to three. Your media rep should be here soon. I'd better be getting back to my office."

Manion felt his heart begin to pound as Lynne got up to leave. An uncomfortable pressure built until he finally blurted out, just as she reached his office door, "Do you have a couple of minutes?"

Lynne turned and looked at him with surprise. "Sure," she replied.

Jim opened a drawer in his desk and started speaking to Donato while he was flipping through some file folders. "I've been working on some new product concepts. We're just about ready to go to test with some of them. Before we spend the money, I'd like to get some more input. Would you mind going over a few briefs?" Manion looked up at Lynne and felt his palms grow cold and damp as he waited for her response.

"No, I don't mind. What exactly do you want me to comment on? . . . Production issues?" she asked.

"Actually, I was hoping you'd play devil's advocate and look for anything that strikes you as odd. Production. Sales. Market statistics. Anything at all. Our last product introduction was a real bonanza for the company. I want to make sure we do everything we can to have another successful launch."

Donato moved to Manion's desk and sat in one of his side chairs. "Let me have a quick look at what I'm getting myself into."

Jim handed her five file folders. "Each of the briefs follows a common format. We're trying to capture only the key points on each brief. That way we can keep them to three pages. Any research, news clippings, and so forth, used in the concept development are noted on the bottom of the last page. If you need any of that material pulled, we can get it for you."

Lynne scanned one of the product briefs. "When do you need these back?"

"Any chance for tomorrow? That way I'll have time to make adjustments to my board presentation."

Donato took out her pocket-size calendar. "I never go anywhere without this. I'm pretty well tied up the balance of the afternoon, and I've got a couple of meetings first thing in the morning, then another two in the afternoon tomorrow."

"What's the best you think you could do?"

"Maybe noon the day after."

"OK, that'll be fine. Do you want me to make photocopies of each of the briefs for you? I can drop them off at your office after I've finished with my three o'clock."

"No, that's not necessary, I can get copies made and have the originals back to you this afternoon." Donato closed her pocket calendar and got up to leave. "Thanks for the help with my visuals for the board meeting and for agreeing to the stint at the community college."

Jim pointed to the file folders Lynne was carrying. "I figure with what's under your arm, we're even."

After Lynne left his office Manion sat and stared at his wall calendar. Carole broke his reverie. "Jim, your three o'clock appointment is here."

"Thanks Carole, send him in please."

■ ■ ■

On the way back to her office Donato met Philippe Fontaine in the hallway.

"How's life treating you?" he asked.

"It's been a little crazy lately," replied Lynne.

"I guess the plant expansion has got you really hopping these days."

"That plus getting ready for the board meeting and planning to increase production in nine weeks. . . . It's busy alright!"

"I hate to ask you this, but is there any chance we could grab a few minutes this afternoon or in the morning? I'd like to get a quick overview on how you see the manufacturing presentation going together for the board meeting," said Philippe.

Donato looked at her watch. "We might as well do it now while the subject is at the top of my mind. I just left a meeting with Carole and Jim where we planned my presentation visuals. How's my office? It's closer."

Lynne guided Fontaine through the flow of her presentation, easily fielding the few pointed questions Philippe threw at her.

"You've done your homework as always, Lynne. The presentation is good and tight, and you've got all the pertinent details at your fingertips. I'm sure the board meeting will be a breeze."

"Thanks, Philippe. I know how important this plant expansion is to the growth of the company. None of us wants to risk losing approval from the board."

"How are you holding up under all the pressure? You've got a lot of balls in the air. . . . Do you feel alright?" asked Philippe.

"I feel fine. Why do you ask?"

Fontaine assumed a more open posture to try to put Donato at ease. "I was speaking to Katherine today after you were in to see her. She sensed that there was something on your mind, but for some reason you chose not to discuss it. I offered to try to find out what was bothering you."

Donato crossed her arms and rotated her chair so that she had her back to Fontaine. "If I told you what was bugging me, would it stay between just the two of us?"

"Lynne, you know I can't give you that kind of carte blanche guarantee," said Fontaine. "It depends on what it is. I'd be legally obligated to take action if it was something like sexual harassment or a discrimination issue. You know I couldn't stand by if it was fraud or some other ethical issue. You'll have to be the judge."

"Well, it's nothing like sexual harassment or fraud."

"Then chances are excellent it could stay just between us."

"It's Manion," said Lynne as she turned back to face Fontaine.

"You had another big blowup with him?"

"No, not at all. In fact our meeting today was very cordial for a change."

"That's a welcome improvement." Philippe sat back and waited for Lynne to continue.

"I heard a rumor that Jim's career is on the line."

"Oh? . . . "

Donato's gaze didn't leave Philippe's face. "I've had to work with him pretty closely over the past three or four years. Jim's done a lot of good things for the company. It upsets me to think . . . " She looked away, her voice trailing off.

"That we'd turn him out to pasture." Fontaine finished her thought.

Lynne looked back at Philippe. "Yes."

Philippe was taken aback. Donato's revelation was unexpected. His mind scrambled for a response.

"I can understand why a rumor like that would upset you. What makes you think there's any substance to it?"

"Circumstantial things . . . Jim's budget getting hammered last week. Katherine having lunch with him after the management committee meeting last Wednesday. Jim not coming back to the office after lunch that day." Donato's stare bored into Philippe. "And your closed-door meeting Wednesday afternoon with Katherine."

Fontaine clasped his hands in his lap. He knew that one of Jim's greatest fears was the rumor mill. Manion was worried that his personal credibility would be destroyed if the details of his meeting with Katherine Fisher became common knowledge. Now Philippe found himself sitting across the desk from one of Manion's peers. Someone who had heard a rumor. Someone who could put the circumstantial jigsaw puzzle together. Philippe moved his chair closer to Donato's desk and angled it toward the door.

"There have been enough closed-door meetings around here lately. No sense in fueling the rumor mill with another one." Fontaine's voice was low and deliberate. He knew he was taking a chance, but Lynne was sharp. If he lied she'd see through it.

"Lynne . . . there have been discussions with Jim Manion. Katherine is concerned about his attitude and the negative effect he's having on the management team lately."

The color drained from Donato's face. Fontaine continued. "No firm decision has been made to cut Manion. He has a clear understanding of what's expected of him and the deadline attached to it. I met with Jim this morning to discuss the situation further. He's actively working on a program to alter his behavior, and I've committed to help him in a variety of ways."

Lynne swallowed hard. "Thanks for telling me. I appreciate that this is confidential, and I'm aware of the personal risk you've taken by sharing this with me. Is there anything I can do to help?"

"Why would you want to? Seems to me that you and

Jim have had some pretty serious disagreements over the past year."

Donato nodded. "Yeah, we have, but I've been thinking about it. Jim went out of his way for me a number of times the first couple of years he was here. Remember when I asked for the supplemental budget to bring some new technology into the plant?"

"He really believed in the project and gave up some of his budget and sacrificed a few programs to help you get the money. That's not the Manion we saw last week."

"No, but it's the Manion I like to remember. That's why I'd like to help."

"Lynne, anyone who cares can give him support, as long as it's subtle. Anything too overt will only feed the rumor mill." Fontaine paused and looked at her. "At the end of the day it really boils down to Manion. He has to want to change."

Fontaine bowed his head and studied his hands as he gently rubbed his palms together. After a moment he angled his head toward Donato. "Jim can never know about our discussion. I just hope he doesn't find out he's the subject of office gossip. . . . It would tear him apart."

Then he sat upright and looked straight at Donato. "Lynne, I've been honest with you, so I'd appreciate it if you'd be honest with me. Did you put together the pieces about Manion, or did you hear this rumor from someone else?"

"Someone else."

"I see." Fontaine closed his eyes and took a deep breath. "How widespread do you think the rumor is at this point?"

Donato looked pensive. She flashed back to her discussion with Ted Wilkinson, reliving every moment in her mind. Finally she responded to Philippe, "My guess is it's not on the mill yet. I think I stumbled on it while it was still in the hypothesis stage."

"You're sure?" Fontaine asked.

Lynne closed her eyes and went over every word of her conversation with Ted again. She replied in a very deliberate tone, "Yes . . . I'm sure."

Philippe got up from his chair. "Thanks Lynne. Let me know if you hear anything else I should be aware of, or if you think of anything I can do to keep this rumor from getting out on the street."

Fontaine's mind was in overdrive as he left Donato's office. One thought kept popping into his head: "I know who's behind this rumor." He clenched his jaw tightly. He could feel his anger rising.

13

THE FRIDAY AFTERNOON TRAFFIC WAS AGONIZINGLY SLOW, yet Jim was enjoying every moment of it. To be stuck in the thick of rush hour was a sure sign that he had met his objective of leaving the office on time. And lately that was one of his primary goals.

"What a week!" he thought. "Who could have predicted the roller-coaster ride I've been on since Monday."

He smiled as he reflected on the events of the past five days. He recalled the anxiety and tension he had felt all day Monday and the horrible feeling that everyone was looking at him, that somehow they all knew about his meeting with Katherine Fisher. Manion chuckled to himself. "If there is such a thing as reincarnation," he thought, "at least I know I don't want to come back as a goldfish. A fishbowl is no place for me."

Then there was Tuesday. In his mind, Jim could vividly picture the red bulb of the thermometer in the relaxation exercise Miller had given him. He could feel himself letting go of the tension in his body as he visualized the mercury descending, and he could still smell the air at the riverside park where he had stopped prior to his meeting with Fontaine. He remembered the way Fontaine had reacted to him and the commitments they had made at the diner.

Manion reached into the pocket of his suit jacket and felt the two magnets Miller had given him. He summoned the visualization and heard the words of the affirmation he had developed for his interactions with Lynne Donato. Then Peter's words came back to him: "It's absolutely critical that you take responsibility for turning your perceptions around, as if you were one of those magnets. Your success is totally dependent on it."

Jim had practiced the exercises extensively. When the opportunity presented itself he was amazed that he was actually able to take a risk and ask Donato for help. She had come through for him, pointing out some areas where the product concepts needed some work, and offering some suggestions for improvement, which Manion incorporated into his board meeting presentation plan.

"That meeting with Lynne had to be the high point of the week," he mused. "Too bad it didn't go as well with Wilkinson."

Manion had approached Ted Wilkinson on Wednesday morning and asked for input on the product concepts. He ran into a brick wall. Jim recalled Ted's comments: "Look Manion, you're the marketing guru. . . . I don't think I can offer any worthwhile suggestions. Besides, I've got my own presentation to finalize. I really don't think I can spare the time to help you out for at least another three or four weeks. We've got some regional meetings coming up after the board meeting, and I've got a number of major account visits planned over the next couple of months. I'd like to help you. Sorry."

Manion was coming up to his freeway exit. He signalled and pulled off. He'd be home in another five or six minutes. "At least I kept my cool and was able to salvage something from the meeting with Wilkinson," he thought.

Manion had pressed the issue with Ted. Eventually Wilkinson suggested that if Manion was adamant about getting some additional input from the field, then he could contact some of the regional sales managers. Manion followed up on the suggestion and spoke to eight of the field people. He faxed each of them the new product briefs and got their input during lengthy telephone conversations on Wednesday afternoon and throughout the day on Thursday. The effort had been rewarded. The perspectives from the field people had helped to fine-tune a number of the product concepts. Manion also came to appreciate the field sales staff as a valuable and underutilized resource.

"I guess Wilkinson's going to be a tough nut to crack. I'll just have to work on it a little bit at a time," thought Manion. "The big thing is to keep an open mind when I'm dealing with him and focus on the positive aspects of his personality."

Manion pulled into his driveway and turned off his car. He sat there for a few minutes and looked at the house and the yard. He and Karen had bought the house over seven years ago. He remembered when he had planted the trees and shrubs. "A lot has happened since we bought this house," he thought. "I wonder how much longer we're going to be here."

Jennifer ran out of the house to greet her father as he came up the walk. Jim bent down and gave her a hug. "Are you ready for some fun this weekend?" he asked. "I thought we could go to the zoo tomorrow."

She squealed her agreement and raced into the house to tell her brother the news. Manion's face broke into a broad smile as he watched Jennifer scamper inside.

Karen was at the kitchen sink. Jim came up from behind her and wrapped his arms around her waist. "How's the sexiest woman in the country doing today?" He held her close and kissed the side of her neck.

Karen turned her head and kissed Jim's left cheek. "She's doing just fine. How was your day?"

"Wonderful, but it's getting better," he replied. Manion released her, draped his jacket and tie over one of the kitchen chairs, then took a vegetable peeler from the drawer and started to help Karen prepare dinner. "On the way home I was thinking about the week. It's been quite a roller-coaster ride."

Karen smiled. "I'd say you came through with flying colors. You must feel pretty good about the progress you've made."

"The board meeting next Wednesday will be the big test. I think we've put together a very impressive presentation. It really depends on how the board reacts."

"I was referring more to your meetings with Philippe and Lynne."

"Yeah, they both went really well. I expected the meeting with Philippe to go well. We've maintained a good rapport over the past year. I never expected such a positive response from Lynne. It was as if she had forgotten the fights we've had the past year. I'm starting to feel I've got a few people in my corner again."

"What do you think happened with Lynne?" asked Karen.

"I've being focusing on her positive traits as Peter suggested and using the visualization and mental rehearsal techniques. I think they've helped me be a little more open with her, although some sarcastic comments still slipped out."

"You've only been practicing the techniques for a few days. You can't expect to change too quickly."

"You're probably right, although being more in touch with my emotions and perceptions does help me slow down and watch my reactions, which makes it easier to keep my negatives in check."

"Well, it's good to hear that the two of you are starting to patch things up. I remember a few years ago you were always talking about how great it was to work with her."

Jim smiled and nodded. "I remember. We were always getting together and bouncing ideas around about improving products and offering customers more value. Lynne's one of the most customer-focused manufacturing people I've ever met. She made it easy for me to alter product concepts to improve production flow and cut manufacturing costs."

"Maybe she's been remembering those times too," Karen said, rinsing some vegetables under the tap then flicking the water from her fingers in Jim's face. "Maybe there are a few people in your corner. . . . You just didn't notice them."

Manion wiped his face with the back of his hand. "I was thinking about doing something a little special with the kids tomorrow. How about taking them to the zoo?"

"The forecast is calling for rain. . . . "

"Anything major?"

"No, just occasional showers."

"Well, let's go then. We can make our own fun. Who cares about the weather." Manion did a pirouette and started dancing across the kitchen floor. "I can do my impression of Gene Kelly . . . singin' in the rain . . . just singin' in the rain . . . "

Karen rolled her eyes and chuckled. Jennifer groaned loudly. Bryan approached his father and tapped him on the shoulder. "I'll give you a hint: don't quit your day job."

"I see," said Jim, "that no one appreciates talent in this household. Well, in that case you two can set the table for dinner." He gave each of the children a tickle then headed upstairs to change.

After putting the children to bed Karen sat down on the sofa next to Jim. "Working on your visualization and affirmation exercises?"

"Not quite yet," Jim replied. "First I do my breathing to

relax." He had his eyes closed. His lower abdomen was expanding and contracting in a deep, regular pattern.

Karen gave him a quick finger poke just above his belt. "Why's your gut moving when you breathe?"

Manion nearly doubled over. "Hey! You could at least warn me!"

"That would take the fun out of it," Karen replied. "You haven't given me the details of these exercises yet."

"I didn't realize you were that interested in them. Do you want me to walk you through what I'm doing?"

"Sure. Maybe I could use these techniques too."

"First you do a deep-breathing exercise to relax. You breathe in through your nose for a count of three, hold it for a count of three, then exhale through your mouth for a count of three."

Karen interrupted. "But why does your gut move?"

Manion grabbed her hands so she couldn't poke him again. "If you ever watch a baby sleeping you'll see that he doesn't expand his rib cage when he breathes. He takes the air in deeply, all the way into the lower part of his lungs so that his abdomen appears to expand. That's how humans breathe in a natural, relaxed state. As adults our abdomens get tightened up from stress, and we get used to taking very short, shallow breaths. We only use a small portion of our lung capacity."

Karen took a deep breath, expanding her rib cage. "You mean you don't like it when I do this?" She flashed a demure smile and turned so as to present Jim with a profile pose.

"I thought you wanted to learn about relaxation, not stimulation."

"Doesn't one follow the other?" she asked.

"That's a distinct possibility." Manion studied his wife for a moment. "Do you really want to learn these exercises?"

"Yes."

"OK. After using the relaxation exercise you then conjure up a positive emotional experience. While that picture is in your head you try to re-create the physical sensations you felt at the time of the original experience. Once you've recaptured the physical sensations, you hold on to them."

"Why do you do that?"

"Because when you attach the physical sensations to the visualization, it has more impact. The visualization will be imprinted in your brain with more power and depth."

"What positive experience do you try to remember?" asked Karen.

"The birth of each of the kids. I try to re-create the feelings I had the first time I held each of them at the hospital," Manion said.

He continued, "So now you're in a relaxed state and you're holding onto these pleasant physical sensations. The next thing you do is picture yourself in a specific situation. The key is that you're creating your own video in your head. You watch yourself behave exactly as you want to behave, not the way you have in the past."

■

Create your own video in your head.
Watch yourself behave exactly as you want
to behave, not the way you have in the past.

■

"You watch yourself?"

"It's as if you had a video camera in your head. You see the scene through your own eyes, through your normal vantage point. You live the experience in your mind, as if it were real. Then you add an affirmation statement to reinforce the image. When you do all the techniques correctly, you end up reprogramming your brain. When the scene starts to play in real life, your brain will overwrite your old behavior pattern with the new one you've been practicing.

Professional athletes have been using relaxation and visualization techniques for decades."

"What does one of these affirmation statements look like?" asked Karen.

Jim thumbed through a few index cards and handed her one. "Here's one I've been working on. I'm trying to change my reaction to Lynne when she starts to point out what could go wrong with one of my projects."

Karen studied the index card. "You haven't labelled this one with Lynne's name, but I can see how you'd use it with a visualization about her." She read the statement: "I feel fantastic when I regularly encourage people to express their viewpoints. I stay calm and keep an open mind, especially when their views differ from mine."

"I picture myself in a meeting where Lynne starts to pick out some of the weak points in one of my projects," said Jim. "Rather than getting upset or defensive, I see myself being genuinely interested in her input. I demonstrate this by asking her to express her views more fully so I can get a better understanding of her perspective. I imagine myself being very open to her suggestions."

"I suppose there's a correct way to write one of these affirmation statements?" Karen asked.

---■---

WIPE out your old behavior.
W focus on what you Want to have happen.
I use the pronoun I to make it a
personal statement.
P make sure the statement is in the
present tense.
E attach a positive emotion to the
statement.

---■---

"It's pretty simple really. Peter used the word *WIPE* to explain it to me. The *W* stands for "want." You need to focus on what you want to have happen, not what you're trying to avoid. The *I* is a reminder to use the pronoun *I*. The statement must be personal to have an impact on you. The *P* is for "present tense." Peter says the key is to have your brain believe that you have already achieved the desired change, so you need to write the statement in the present tense. Finally, the *E* stands for "emotion." It's critical to attach a positive emotion to the statement. That way it gets imprinted in your brain with more impact."

"That's where the word *fantastic* comes in. . . . "

"Exactly. The word *WIPE* is an ideal way to remember the proper structure of an affirmation statement. After all, you're trying to wipe your old behavior out of your mind."

Jim took the affirmation card back from Karen. "I'm only working on three visualizations at the moment. Peter told me to limit the number at first. That way I'll have a better chance of getting them imprinted more quickly."

Karen tossed her head back, sending her hair over her left shoulder. She raised her eyebrows at Jim several times. "So . . . what scene do you visualize me in?"

14

It was the Monday before the board meeting and five days since Philippe Fontaine had learned that a rumor about Manion might be about to surface. He had been able to control his emotions after his meeting with Lynne, but the thought of such a rumor had eaten at him for the rest of the week. The little voice in his head kept telling him that Wilkinson was behind the rumor. But Philippe knew he had nothing concrete to go on because Lynne had not volunteered her source.

He had made himself a promise as he left work on Friday: if on Monday he still felt uneasy about the potential that a rumor would surface, he'd discuss the matter with Katherine Fisher. By nine Monday morning he was on his way to her office.

"Good morning, Katherine, have you had a coffee yet?"

"As a matter of fact I haven't. I got in a little late this morning, and I was just about to go get one. Do you want to join me?" she replied.

"Better than that, I'll buy . . . as long as we go out for one."

Katherine was somewhat surprised by Philippe's request, but she knew he wouldn't have asked if it weren't important. "Your car or mine?"

"Not only will I buy, I'll even drive," Philippe said.

On the way to the local coffee shop the two exchanged small talk about their weekend activities. Katherine seemed more poised than she had the previous week.

Once seated in the coffee shop, Philippe took the opportunity to question Fisher about the two exercises she had completed for him the previous week.

"Did you have any more thoughts about the descriptions you wrote about Manion and your relationship with him?"

After sipping her coffee pensively Katherine replied, "Those were good exercises, Philippe. I didn't get any huge revelations, but every day since then I've had almost a continual series of little pin pricks. I keep recalling little things I've done, quite innocently, that Jim could have misread. Things that could have put him on the defensive."

"It doesn't take much, does it?" Fontaine added.

"No, it doesn't. I began to realize that what you actually say to someone is such a small portion of your total communication with them. We all send so many other signals."

"And people are sensitive to nonverbal communication whether they realize it or not," said Philippe. "We all need to be careful to monitor what messages we're sending out."

"Philippe, before I did the first exercise in which you asked me to describe Manion, I didn't realize how my attitude toward him had changed. Then, when you had me do the second one and describe my relationship with Jim, it became apparent that my attitudes toward him had carried over and created a negative impact on our relationship as well."

Katherine's finger circled the top of her coffee cup. "As a manager you forget that the most important parts of your job are encouraging your people to perform up to their potential and giving them the tools they need to succeed.

When they don't perform well, you have to stop and look in the mirror and realize you shoulder some of the responsibility."

As a manager the most important parts of your job are encouraging your people to perform up to their potential and giving them the tools they need to succeed.

Fontaine smiled warmly. "We all need to take stock of ourselves, Katherine, but let's not get off track. I think the bottom line with Jim is still pretty much the same. He knows what he has to do and how much time he has to get it done. You had some impact on his behavior, we all did, but it's still up to him to make the necessary changes. One of the things I wanted to talk to you about was some positive signs I'm starting to see."

"Like what?"

"Manion had a meeting with Donato to go over her board presentation material. When I saw Lynne last week she commented that the meeting was very cordial and constructive."

"Well, that's a start. The two of them have had a couple of problems during the past nine months. By the way, did you have an opportunity to find out whether there's something bothering her?"

"Yes I did. I just haven't been sure how to deal with it."

Katherine sipped her coffee and waited for Fontaine to continue.

"She threw me a real curveball. She said she had heard a rumor that Manion's career was on the line. It upset her quite a bit."

"She said *what!*"

"She said she heard a rumor that Manion was going to be fired."

Katherine sank back in her chair and looked stunned. "Where would she get something like that?"

"It's based on circumstantial things. Manion's budget getting slashed. Your lunch with him after the management committee meeting. Manion not returning from lunch that day. The closed-door meeting you and I had."

Fisher shook her head. "I can't believe Lynne would take note of all those events and put them together to draw that kind of a conclusion. It's not like her to speculate on office politics."

"She didn't. Apparently someone came to her with the scenario. She thinks it was hypothesis testing."

"By whom?"

"I didn't ask, and she didn't volunteer. A little voice in my head has been telling me for the past five days that it was Ted," Fontaine said. "I have absolutely no proof. I just keep getting this strong message that it was him."

Fisher crossed her arms over her chest then brought her hand up to her chin. "I don't want to go on a witch-hunt, but I have to admit that if I were to pick someone, it would be Ted." Katherine took a deep breath. "If that rumor actually got into circulation and Jim found out . . . "

They sat motionless, considering the consequences. Finally Katherine continued, "It could sabotage Jim's chances for making a turnaround. He'd naturally blame at least one of us for the leak. We'd both lose credibility with him." Katherine shook her head and grew silent.

Fontaine spoke. "That's the dilemma that I've been struggling with. It's not like the rumor's out. At this point we only have a strong potential for one. If we press Donato for the source, we compromise her and jeopardize our relationships with her. Besides, you can't fire someone for starting office gossip."

"Maybe you can't fire someone like Ted, but you could put him on warning. After all, that kind of stunt shows a complete lack of professionalism," replied Katherine. "Especially when the rumor comes out of management ranks. It really points to an immature, insecure personality. I'll bet most employees have no idea how much their careers can be damaged when rumors are traced back to them. You just can't promote people who play those kinds of stupid games."

Most employees have no idea how much their careers can be damaged when rumors are traced back to them.

"I suppose the issue at this point is what, if anything, can we do?"

"I agree with you, Philippe. We can't force Donato to reveal where she heard it. We can't tell Jim, or we would seriously jeopardize his chances of pulling off a successful turnaround. We can't go by our instincts and talk to Wilkinson. If we've guessed wrong, we send him a pretty negative message about what we think of him. If we guess right, then we confirm his suspicions. Then his hypothesis will come out into the open as more than just a rumor. Then it would be fact. Dealing with this thing is like trying to fight a shadow."

Fontaine cast his gaze out into the parking lot for a few minutes. A smile started to appear on his face. "There is one thing we can do."

Fisher looked at him expectantly.

"We've been trying to come up with a solution by working through formal channels. This type of communication travels on the informal network. We have to combat it at that level."

"And how do we do that?" Katherine asked.

"I mentioned earlier that Lynne was quite upset by the rumor. She seems to genuinely want to help Jim. Why don't we ask her to send a message back up the informal channel to the source of the rumor?" said Philippe.

"What might that message be?" asked Fisher.

"A very simple message. We ask Lynne to tell the source that she thinks this rumor is potentially very damaging to not only Manion, but the company as well. Then she tells the source that if she hears the rumor surface anywhere in the company, she will report the source to senior management."

"Would Lynne do it?" asked Katherine.

"If she thought it was the only way to help Manion, she might."

"OK, let's assume she does. Would it work on the source?"

"Put yourself in the source's shoes," Philippe said. "The rumor mill only works because it's clandestine. No one is held accountable for the trash that is created. To have a respected member of the management team, a vice president, finger you . . . unless you have a death wish why would you risk spreading the rumor?"

Katherine sat motionless, her eyes in tight focus on Philippe. "OK. See if Donato will do it."

15

AFTER RETURNING FROM THE COFFEE SHOP WITH PHILIPPE Fontaine, Katherine decided to call an afternoon meeting of the management committee to review the board presentations. She quickly composed an e-mail message requesting that all the committee members meet at two o'clock that afternoon.

As she sorted through her morning mail, Fisher found herself thinking about her conversation with Philippe and his speculation that Wilkinson was behind the potential rumor. The more she dwelled on the issue, the more episodes Katherine remembered that supported Fontaine's judgment.

"Ted's nose has been a bit out of joint ever since Manion got here," she thought. Wilkinson had made it clear on a couple of occasions in the past that he thought the marketing function should have been put under him. Katherine also knew that Ted was a little put out because he hadn't made vice president.

Katherine had never considered an executive promotion for Ted. She thought his parlor humor and penchant for sarcasm showed a certain degree of immaturity. Wilkinson had risen to the position of national sales manager because he dealt well with the company's major accounts and was able to get solid performance from the field staff. In short, he delivered the numbers.

Fisher knew that Ted had a reputation for being something of a gossip hound. Early on in his career he had received a reprimand for that very sin. Katherine also realized that she was a little guarded when she was around Wilkinson. Too often he spoke as if he knew what was going on in the inside track, whether he did or not. He also had an uncanny ability to lead a conversation in a particular direction so that he could either confirm or deny certain suspicions. It was that last point that really had Katherine convinced that Wilkinson was behind the Manion rumor.

Fisher's telephone called for some attention. She picked it up on the second ring.

"Hello Katherine, it's Philippe. I had a chat with Lynne Donato this morning. I put our cards on the table regarding the options available to senior management."

"What was her reaction?"

"Mixed. I think she fully understands the predicament we face and the impact the rumor might have on Manion's attempt to get himself turned around. On the other hand, I'm not sure she's at all comfortable taking an aggressive stance with the source," Philippe said.

"How did you leave it with her?" asked Fisher.

"Basically I put the ball squarely in her court. I told her that there were too many risks for you and me even to attempt to use formal channels to deal with the issue. I told Lynne that she was the only person in a position to kill the rumor before it surfaced," Fontaine answered. "I also told her that time was running out. If she was going to act, it would need to be soon."

"That's all you could have done. What are the chances she'll take action?"

Philippe pondered the question for a few moments. "Fifty-fifty," he replied.

"Well, that's better odds than we had this morning. Thanks for handling that, Philippe. See you at two o'clock."

That afternoon Katherine looked around the conference table at the management committee. "Let's go over the structure and the basic approaches we'll be using at the board meeting on Wednesday."

She placed a transparency on the overhead projector and reviewed the agenda for the upcoming meeting. "As you can see, each of you has between fifteen to thirty minutes for presenting prepared material, as well as an additional fifteen minutes to handle questions from the board. Make sure I have copies of your handouts before you leave the office today."

Katherine scanned the room quickly. "Any questions at this point? OK. Let's follow the presentation order on the agenda. I'd like each of you to give the group a summary of the key points you plan to make in your presentation. Keep the summary short, maybe three to five minutes. After each summary I'd like the group to try to come up with at least six questions board members are likely to ask. As we come up with questions pertinent to your area, be prepared to respond to them. Let's make sure to write down all the questions and our responses. I'd like overheads prepared to cover these supplemental issues. That way if any of these questions surface, we'll be able to handle them professionally."

As each member of the group encapsulated his or her presentation, Katherine's comfort level rose. Everyone was well prepared and focused on the key issues. The questions posed by group members after each presentation were insightful and demanding, and Fisher was pleased with the responses.

She paid special attention to Donato, Wilkinson, and Manion. Katherine felt sure that if there was going to be a snag at the board meeting, it would be about the plant expansion and the company's sales and marketing efforts.

"I notice you've changed some of the new product concepts quite a bit since we saw them last week, Jim. Why have you done that?" she asked.

"There are some good reasons, Katherine. Lynne looked over the final briefs and pointed out that making some product modifications would streamline our production methods and lower our costs. Plus we'd have better quality control. By making the manufacturing process more efficient we think we'll improve our chances of meeting our customers' expectations as well as maximizing our profits."

Katherine nodded her head in agreement. "I also see that you've made some changes in the launch strategy."

"Yes we did. That comes from a couple of things we did. First, we got the marketing team together to review, in detail, our last major product launch. We didn't want to waste marketing resources by reinventing the wheel if we didn't have to. In the revised launch strategy we're reusing approaches that worked well in the past. We did an analysis to ensure that the approaches are relevant for the new products. Then we spent a lot of time going over what we could have done better with the last product launch two years ago. Our goal was to learn from our past mistakes and use the lessons on this launch."

"That's good, Jim. The only other question I have is about the regional sales forecasts. They've changed pretty dramatically in a few areas. I'm not complaining. . . . It's nice to see higher sales projections," Fisher said.

Wilkinson had just picked up on the changes Manion had made to the sales figures. His eyes were riveted to the overhead screen while the heel of his right foot tapped nervously on the floor. As he reviewed the figures a slight smirk crept over his face. He jotted some notes on his pad.

"Those aren't pie-in-the-sky numbers, Katherine," replied Manion. "In a discussion I had with Ted he suggested that it would be prudent to contact some of the regional sales managers for their input."

Wilkinson's head abruptly turned away from the overhead screen and toward Jim. He put down his pen.

Jim continued. "When we did that we found that three out of the eight regional folks we surveyed felt very strongly that the new products would have better market appeal than we first thought. We focused on those three initial regional managers then polled some of the neighboring ones. It turned out that there were distinct areas of the country where all the regional managers felt very optimistic about the new products. We asked them to give us some details on why they were so optimistic."

Manion picked up a file folder, took out the contents, and dropped the stack of reports on the table for effect. "Ted's people were very thorough and prompt with their feedback. The result is that we're going to be able to do an effective job of micromarketing in key geographic areas as well as in the national launch. This double-barreled approach should catch our competitors napping. We never would have come up with the strategy without Ted's idea and the input from his field people."

Katherine smiled broadly at Manion then gave a positive nod to Wilkinson. "It's nearly five o'clock folks. Unless there are any other questions or concerns we should wrap this up. Thanks everyone. . . . This should be one heck of a board meeting Wednesday."

Philippe and Katherine gathered up their material slowly, letting the rest of the management committee filter out of the room.

"Did you catch it?" asked Philippe.

"There was lots to catch."

"The stares between Donato and Wilkinson were so frozen you could hang your laundry on them," said Fontaine.

"Mission accomplished?" asked Fisher.

"I think so."

16

THE FOLLOWING WEDNESDAY AFTERNOON KATHERINE could feel the elation building as she stood in the lobby watching the board members file out of the building to their waiting cars. As she turned to rejoin the members of her senior team she winked at the receptionist, tapping her knuckles on her workstation and saying, "It's been a good day, Amy. A very good day."

Manion and the rest of the management team were still gathering up their materials when Katherine reentered the boardroom. They all looked up and turned toward her.

"You all did a magnificent job today," she said. "Your presentations were superb, and your responses to the board members' questions were very focused and professional." A broad smile broke out on her face. "There's no way we would have gotten approval for the plant expansion without your efforts today. Way to go folks!" Fisher continued, looking directly at Manion, "And it was great to see some of the old teamwork coming back. Thanks everybody."

The room buzzed as the management team exchanged congratulatory handshakes. Wilkinson was the first to leave, walking out of the room abruptly and looking somewhat tense. When Manion returned to his office he picked up the telephone and dialed seven digits he had committed to memory.

"Hey, Peter, what's on for the weekend?" he asked.

"It's time to recharge my batteries, so I'm going to settle down with a couple of good books and make some time to go for a long walk in the woods."

"Sounds like a perfect weekend," Jim said.

"Wasn't your board meeting today?"

"Just got out of it."

"How did it go?"

"Fantastic! Lynne did an incredible job with her presentation, so we were able to get the plant expansion budget approved. She got grilled pretty well by the board, but she handled all of their questions without missing a beat."

"That's great! What about your marketing plans for the new products you've been working on?"

"They also went through without a hitch. You were right about Lynne. I asked her to take a critical look at the plans, and she came back with some excellent suggestions, which I used. I doubt if the plans would have been accepted so readily by the board if it hadn't been for her input and the feedback I got from sales," said Jim.

"You got some help from Wilkinson?" Peter sounded surprised.

"No, not on a personal basis. But I did get him to agree that I could get some input directly from the regional sales managers. Their perspectives really helped. Most of them were quite tentative at first. They seemed shocked to be asked for their ideas. But it didn't take long for them to open up. I got some great input from them."

"You were anticipating a few sticky points about current sales volumes. Did they materialize?" asked Peter.

"The issue came up alright," said Jim. "Wilkinson had brought some material showing the cyclical nature of our markets. As usual, a couple of the board members didn't want to accept past sales curves as predictors for the future. I waited until they were pressing the issue pretty hard before I played our ace in the hole," Manion explained.

"Trying to be a superstar, were you?" teased Miller.

Jim chuckled. "Not at all. When you have only one ace, you want to make sure it gets played at the right time. Remember how I surveyed some of the regional sales managers the week before the board meeting?"

"Uh-huh."

"At the end of each conversation I asked our sales people to update me if any large orders were placed, especially if they came from some of our seasonal accounts. I explained to them that the information could be extremely helpful during the board meeting. I made sure they understood the WIIFM."

"WIIFM?" Peter said in a puzzled voice.

"The world's most popular radio station . . . WII-FM—what's in it for me. That's the only reason most people do anything," Jim answered.

---

*D*etermine your WIIFM— what's in it for me?

"A large part of the compensation package for our sales people is driven by a sliding commission scale. By reinforcing how the plant expansion and our upcoming product launches would increase their sales volumes and move them up to higher commission levels I was able to get some of the sales people to see that what we do at corporate is designed to help them—not just give them more work."

"They think corporate's there to help them? Now that's what I call a breakthrough!" quipped Miller.

"Anyway, as it happened, four or five of our field people called me with details on some major deals that were confirmed just before the board meeting. I knew that we could get past the sales issue with the board if we used the information at the right time. For some reason Ted neglected to mention the deals when he was responding to questions from the board. I sensed that the mood was beginning to turn. I waited as long as I could before addressing the issue."

"You brought up the late-breaking deals?" asked Peter.

"Yes, I had no choice given the way the meeting was going."

"Did you upstage Wilkinson?"

"That was the hardest part, using the field sales information without making Wilkinson look bad. After all, as the national sales manager he not only should have had the information at his fingertips; he should have used it."

"How did you introduce the information?" Peter asked.

"One of the board members asked Ted a very pointed question about several of our biggest cyclical accounts. They wanted to know why Ted thought we'd retain the business from those specific accounts. By sheer coincidence the three accounts mentioned had all placed significant orders just before the board meeting. I assumed that since the regional folks told me about the orders, they would have told Ted too. Anyway, the room was dead quiet while everyone waited for Ted to reply. It became obvious to me that either Wilkinson had forgotten about the orders or he didn't know about them yet, so I spoke up," explained Manion.

"That must have been a very touchy moment. How did you handle it?" asked Peter.

"I simply told the board that Ted had mentioned the orders to me over coffee that morning. Then I gave them the details I had about the size and values of the various orders. Ted recovered quickly after that point and picked up the ball. He filled in some details about the sales programs his people were using with the accounts. I think it came across as nothing more than a momentary lapse on Ted's part. The discussion then moved on to other areas."

"What was Wilkinson's reaction?"

"At first he appeared to be relieved to be helped out of a jam. But by the end of the board meeting he was giving me looks to kill," replied Manion. "He got the credit for the late-breaking sales information, so he looked good to the board and our management team. You'd think he'd be happy about that, especially since I don't think he had a clue about the orders."

"Why do you think he didn't?" asked Miller.

"I noticed he was making notes about the deals as I was describing them to the board. After the meeting he was very abrupt with me and made a comment about getting more timely information from the field. He was the first one to leave the room after Katherine congratulated us, and he looked like a pressure cooker under full boil."

"If you're right that Wilkinson didn't know, it probably means that some of his regional sales folks gave you information that they purposely didn't give him, putting him at a serious disadvantage during the meeting. No wonder he was fuming."

"It looks like there are some serious problems in the sales department," replied Jim.

"And you, my friend, may have stumbled into a hornet's nest."

"Believe me, Peter, I'm not going to touch this issue with a ten-foot pole. The regional sales people obviously have their reasons for doing what they did. Given the situation I'm facing at work, the last thing I need to do is get involved with politics in another department."

"You may not have much of a choice," Peter said.

"What do you mean?"

"Most people in a corporate environment realize that information is power. By giving you information before giving it to their superior through official channels, those regional sales managers could be sending you a message that they want help. They may be looking for an ally outside their department. Sometimes the easiest way to form an alliance is to barter for it with information."

"It could be they're just trying to be helpful."

Miller's voice was deliberate. "Possible but not probable. Remember that it looks as if they gave you the information before giving it to their boss. They knew that the information could be critical and that it might be used during one of the most important board meetings of the year. They also knew that if the information came out through you, their boss might look bad. People don't take that kind of a risk without a reason. A good reason."

Miller paused noticeably. "What are you going to do if Wilkinson nails his people to the cross for helping you?"

"I don't know."

"Unless you don't care what's going to happen to those regional sales managers, you'd better think about what you're going to do, and pretty quickly."

"Of course I care what's going to happen to them. . . . " Manion's voice trailed off as he remembered the look on Ted's face as he left the meeting. "I imagine Wilkinson is already addressing this issue."

"You can bet he is! Jim, those regional guys need to know that they're going to get support from you."

Manion shook his head. "Goddamnit! I get one little victory under my belt with the meeting today, and now I'm facing a potentially huge blowout with Ted. How am I supposed to deal with that when Fisher's expecting more cooperative behavior from me?"

"Look, maybe there's a way you can deal with this so it doesn't turn into a battle between you and Ted. The first thing you need to do is make sure you understand what you're dealing with," Peter said.

"You're right. I'll call the regional folks who gave me the

information and thank them for making the extra effort to call me back. I'll let them know that I used what they gave me and that it really helped to make the board meeting successful. If they want to share anything else with me, my call will give them the opportunity. Then I'll have to figure out what to do about it."

"Jim, you're obviously facing a tough situation," said Peter. "Remember to ask yourself, 'What do I have to understand?' before you ask 'What should I do?'"

"And I could add another question in the middle: 'What am I trying to achieve?'" replied Manion.

When facing a tough situation, ask yourself three questions: What do I need to understand? What am I trying to achieve? What do I need to do?

"That's the project manager in you coming out."

"Speaking of project management, did I mention that Donato asked me to speak to the marketing students at her college?"

"No, you didn't."

"Yeah, on the fourteenth. She wants me to talk to the students about how to apply project management principles to marketing communications."

"Well, she picked the right person. You're the best I've ever seen," said Peter.

"Thanks. I think it should be a lot of fun, and I hope the students can get something out of it," said Manion as he glanced at his watch. "I have to go, Peter. I've still got those five calls to make to the regional sales managers."

"Good luck. Let me know what happens."

17

AFTER BEING INTRODUCED BY AN ASSOCIATE MARKETING professor from the community college, Jim Manion stood up and faced his audience. He looked out into the lecture hall and saw one hundred and seventy pairs of eyes staring back at him.

Manion unbuttoned his suit jacket and moved out from the podium area. He placed his notes and a duffel bag on a table next to the overhead projector and began speaking to the students. "Before I get into the meat of my presentation, I'd like to ask you a few questions. How many people in the room are enrolled in the college and are taking this advanced marketing course so they can pursue a career in advertising?"

Almost 80 percent of the students raised their hands.

Jim strolled out into the audience. "Why do you want to be in advertising?" he asked. Manion stared at a pocket of about a dozen students, forcing them to respond.

"It's always been a dream of mine."

"The money is fantastic."

"It's a glamourous career."

"A plush office."

"I've always been creative."

Manion continued to stroll through the room, eliciting more responses. Finally he singled out one student wearing a big smirk. "And you?" he asked.

"Use my talent. Make it big and live the good life" was the reply.

Jim turned around and ambled back toward the table next to the overhead projector, speaking as he went. "OK. Who would rather have a career in which sixty hours is a short workweek? A career where the whole world sees every mistake you make, no matter how small? A career where you'll start out making eighteen to twenty thousand a year, twenty-five if you're really lucky? A career in which abusive clients are legendary?"

Manion turned casually to face his audience. "And if you're better than average, you'll stay in the industry for eight to ten years. After that you'll have to change careers because nobody will want you anymore."

The room was quiet. Jim raised his right arm. "Show of hands, please." No one in the hall moved a muscle. "Folks, welcome to the exciting world of advertising." He took off his suit jacket and began his presentation.

For the next hour Manion kept the audience riveted with his insights, humor, and real-life experiences. He described a number of processes used to develop advertising campaigns and the traditional relationship between agencies and their clients. He then went on to explain how campaigns go awry. Jim then began the second half of his presentation.

"The statistics aren't promising. Let's not kid ourselves. Few of you will have the opportunity to make a living in the advertising business. Even fewer will stay in the field for the bulk of your careers. Many of you who do use your talents and prosper in the business may fall victim to its pressures. You'll face divorce. Drug and alcohol abuse. Maybe worse."

Every student's gaze was frozen on Manion. "For the

next hour I want to share some information with you that everyone in this room can use. Regardless of the career path you end up on. Regardless of the industry you work in. Regardless of where you end up in the hierarchy of an organization. If you use what I'm going to share with you during the next hour, your chances of success will be greatly increased."

Jim walked over to the overhead, placed a transparency on it, and flicked on the lamp switch. The machine projected a type image on the screen: PROJECT MANAGEMENT.

"From this moment on I want all of you to consider yourselves as being in the change management business. Whatever your job, whatever challenges you face, the reason you'll be paid in the future will be based on how well you can adapt to and manage change."

---■---------■---

The reason you'll be paid in the future will be based on how well you can adapt to and manage change.

---■---------■---

Manion motioned to the overhead image. "Project management is a disciplined way of dealing with change. It doesn't have to be complicated. It doesn't need to be full of fancy jargon that no one can remember. What it needs to be is something you can relate to on an everyday basis. It needs to be a tool you can use to focus your efforts and generate consistently high levels of performance. It's one of two things you'll need to be successful. We'll talk about the other thing you'll need in a few minutes."

Jim took a jigsaw puzzle box out of his duffel bag and walked toward the audience. "Since the majority of you are interested in advertising, we'll relate the project management principles directly back to the field where we can." He held up the puzzle box. "And we'll use a few other things to help illustrate the concepts."

Manion walked up to a student in the front row and dumped the contents of the puzzle box on her desk. Then he nonchalantly tossed the puzzle box backward toward the overhead projector. "Would you mind helping me out by putting this puzzle together?"

The student looked up at him, obviously perplexed. "I can't," she said.

"Why not?"

"I don't know what the puzzle is supposed to look like."

"No problem. It has a red barn, green trees, and three cows on it," Manion said. "Can you do it now?"

She shook her head no.

"Why not?"

"I have no idea how big the barn is, where the cows are in the picture, or anything about the trees, their color, size. . . . "

"What would you need to be able to do the puzzle?" Manion asked.

"The puzzle box."

"Why?"

"Then I would know exactly what the picture was supposed to look like."

Jim smiled at her then looked out at the rest of the audience. "What we have just witnessed is the importance of having a very specific objective. How can we start working on a project if we don't know what the exact objective is? The answer is simple: we can't."

Manion walked over to the puzzle box, picked it up off the floor, and asked the student to put the pieces back in the box. "Who can give me some objectives we might establish for advertising?"

Several students raised their hands. Jim moved in front

of a flip chart and pointed to the students in turn. "Go ahead."

"To increase brand awareness."

"To improve the brand image."

"To generate interest in a product."

"To inform the public."

Manion jotted down their ideas for all to see. He thanked the students for their input then said, "These are pretty typical objectives we're apt to see in most advertising plans. Unfortunately every one of them is useless."

Murmurs ran through the audience. Jim continued, "Don't get me wrong. These are all valid reasons why we'd advertise. They just don't represent valid objectives. A good objective has to identify a target in very precise terms. It must describe where you are now, where you want to go, and how much time you have to get there."

He moved over to the overhead projector, changed the transparency, and read the new one out loud: "A good objective states from where to where by when." He turned to face the audience. "It makes sense, doesn't it?" he asked. "You need to know where you're starting from, and where you're going to, before you start something. And you need to know when you need to arrive. When you go on a trip, you don't just wander around aimlessly. You have a destination in mind and an estimated time of arrival."

■

A good objective states from where to where by when.

■

The students nodded their silent agreement.

Manion continued. "Let's take the first objective you suggested—to increase brand awareness. Do we know our starting point? How much awareness we want to create? When we want to create it by? No. We have no way of assessing how much advertising we need to run, or even where to run it based on this original statement. Let's take this statement and rework it so that it becomes measurable."

"Let's say this was our OBJECTIVE." Jim put up a new transparency and read it. "To increase top of mind, unaided brand awareness from the current level of 11 percent to 15 percent within eighteen months, our target audience being males aged twenty-five to thirty-four with incomes over forty thousand."

Manion walked back toward the audience. "Do we know from where? Sure . . . 11 percent. To where? Yes . . . 15 percent. By when? Of course, . . . eighteen months."

Manion walked back to the table next to the overhead projector. He reached down into his duffel bag and pulled out a road sign and held it up for the audience to see. "After you've established a good, tight objective you need to look at your project just like this sign: ROAD CLOSED," he said.

Jim walked toward the students, holding the ROAD CLOSED sign in front of him. "Before we can effectively plan out a project, we need to identify all the roadblocks ahead of us, all the reasons why the road may be closed. First we look at external issues such as government regulations, competitive products, market conditions, and so on. Then we look at internal factors and assess our organization. What are the skills of our people? What is our production and engineering capability? What is the extent of our distribution channel? . . . We look at anything that might restrict the success of our project."

Manion scanned the room, making eye contact as he continued to move closer toward the audience. "We must identify all the limiting factors our project must overcome if it is to be successful. This step is key to helping us to break the project down into functional areas."

Manion turned around and returned to the stage. "Think about our jigsaw puzzle. You just don't sit down and start putting a puzzle together, do you? No. You start by deciding where your work area will be, how much light you need, whether you have the patience needed to complete the puzzle. It's only after you do these basic things that you actually start to work on the puzzle. Do you start by grabbing random pieces and putting them together? Of course

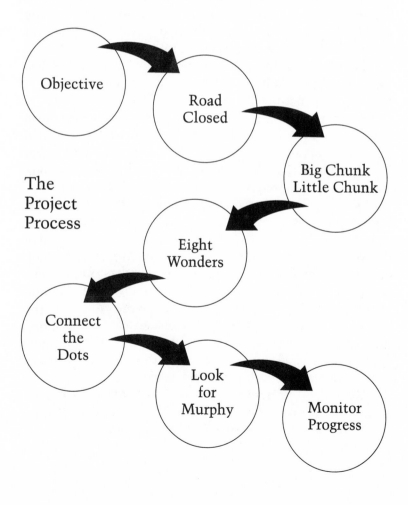

not. You start by sorting the various pieces by color. You put all the green pieces together. The brown pieces. The blue pieces. After that you start to assemble separate areas of the puzzle. It's the same thing with any project."

Jim wrote on a new page of the flip chart as he spoke. "First we break it down into BIG CHUNKS. With a communication program that could be national advertising, sales promotion, trade shows, and press activities. Then we break the BIG CHUNKS DOWN INTO LITTLE CHUNKS. For example, you could break national advertising down into media buying, production, and creative development. Sometimes you may even break the little chunks down into even smaller pieces. Under production that could be television, billboard, newspaper, magazine, radio, dealer co-op, and so on. The trick is to remember these words from Henry Ford."

Manion displayed an overhead transparency that read: THERE HAS NEVER BEEN A TASK THAT COULD NOT BE DONE AS LONG AS IT WAS BROKEN DOWN INTO SMALL ENOUGH PIECES.

"Keep breaking the project down until you eventually get to an easily managed series of individual tasks. Now you can determine how much time and money the project is going to take. Has anyone heard of the Seven Wonders of the World?"

Most of the students raised their hands. "I want everyone to remember that there are also 'wonders' in planning out a project. But there's eight not seven. Eight simple questions you need to answer for each part of the project. Think of yourself as a news reporter. You have to ask all the correct questions if you want to write a good story. It's the same thing with a good project. You need to get answers to the right questions for each part of the project."

Manion put up another overhead transparency titled THE EIGHT WONDERS OF THE WORLD. He revealed the questions one at a time and offered his explanation for each.

"*Why is this chunk necessary?* One of the best ways to

improve the cost and time performance of any project is to identify and eliminate unnecessary work. This first question does that for us.

"*What measurable performance do we want from this chunk?* The only way we will know if a particular piece of the project has been successfully completed is if we quantify what performance we expect of it. This also helps us at the end of the entire project when we're trying to learn how we can improve our performance in the future. We can look for individual performance gaps—either positive or negative—in the execution of the plan, and then figure out why we performed at that level.

"*What skills and attitudes will the person doing this chunk need?* This question helps us identify the ideal person for the task from an attitudinal perspective. It also helps us identify the skills training necessary for the person to successfully complete this chunk of the project.

"*Who is going to do this chunk?* Here we establish single point accountability for each chunk of the project. When people are accountable for something, they almost always get it done.

"*What tasks need to be done to complete this chunk?* Often we don't stop to take the time to fully work out all the steps needed to complete a particular chunk of the project. That's why we often get off track with our completion date and cost for the project.

"*Where is this chunk going to be done?* This question helps us determine the exact location for the various types of work that will be done. If we're going to need to work at multiple plants or if some of the work is going to be done off-site, we shouldn't overlook the time and costs of transportation.

"*How long will it take to do this chunk, and when does it need to be finished?* At this stage we need to get input from the person responsible for doing this chunk of the project. That individual needs to commit to a completion date as well as an estimate of how long their chunk will take to finish.

"How much is this chunk going to cost? You'd think this fundamental question would be automatically answered. Not so. Often projects are planned with an overall budget, not broken down into component pieces. If we want to maintain effective cost control for a project, we need to keep track of expenditures for each stage of the project."

Manion turned off the overhead projector and faced the students. "You need to answer all eight questions for each little chunk of the project. When you add up the answers for all the little chunks, you get the cost and time needed for each big chunk. The total for all the big chunks is the budget and time needed for the entire project. Is everybody with me so far?"

Jim took a few steps toward the students to gauge their reaction. Satisfied with their response he continued.

"Now we've finally arrived at the spot where we can decide whether we should actually do the project. We go back to our original objective and assess whether the time and money involved in taking on the project is worth it in terms of a return. That makes sense, doesn't it?"

Virtually all the students in the room raised their hands. Jim continued, "Assuming the budget and time schedule are acceptable, this is the next project stage, folks . . . CON-NECT THE DOTS. We simply take all the individual project tasks and figure out in what order they need to be done. We also check to see which tasks are dependent on other ones."

Manion turned on the overhead projector and put a new graphic on it. It showed a chart with four columns. "A good way of doing this is to simply construct a chart showing all the individual tasks that need to be done."

Jim pointed to the columns in order. "In the first column we list the *tasks*. In the next we assign each task a *number*. Next under the *time* column we put down how many days or hours the task will take. It's important to keep a common measurement of time. Don't mix hours, days, and weeks. The last column is entitled COMPLETION ORDER. This is where you list, in order, the code number of the tasks that must be finished before this one can be started. Once you have the chart finished you use that information to CONNECT THE DOTS. At this point that means draw a flow chart for your project."

Manion continued to speak as he removed the overhead transparency and replaced it with a new one. "Obviously if you have a very large project you would never do a flow chart manually. There's excellent project management software available that will do it for you. To manage the project you need to be able to manage the people who are accountable for little chunks and big chunks. *Make up a chart that details who is responsible* for each task."

He turned again to the audience. "Raise your hand if you've ever been a victim of Murphy's Law." A sea of arms waved in response. "I think the main reason why Murphy's Law is so widely in evidence is because we never think about Murphy beforehand. So our next project stage is to LOOK FOR MURPHY. We go over our flow chart and figure out all the places where Murphy could show up. In essence, what could go wrong. Then we determine how likely it is that Murphy will show up, and if he does, what are the consequences apt to be. We can then *rework the plan to try to eliminate the possibility that Murphy will appear,* or at least to reduce the risk."

Manion pulled a small fire extinguisher out of his duffel bag and held it up to the audience. "Looking for Murphy is nothing more than taking the time to plan our alternatives. That way we won't have to use one of these to fight fires later on."

Manion put the fire extinguisher down on the table. "Let's recap the process quickly. First we identify our target and set a measurable objective that states from where to where by when. We examine why the road to our project might be closed by internal and external factors. Then we break the project down into chunks. We call on the Eight Wonders of the World to help us ask the correct questions about each chunk of the project so we can determine the time and money needed to complete the project. We also spell out the whys, whos, whens, etcetera, of each chunk. Then we connect the dots and create a flow chart, see what could go wrong by looking for Murphy, and rework the plan if necessary. Is everyone comfortable so far?"

When he witnessed a chorus of agreement, Jim continued. "At this point management gives you the go-ahead on the project and you start work. It's absolutely critical to keep track of your actual time and expenses for each little chunk as you go along. Keeping the little chunks under control keeps the entire project under control."

Manion went to the flip chart and drew an XY-axis. "We can map out our budget and time performance on a graph. Let's say that according to our plan, after the first chunk of a seven-chunk project we're supposed to have spent fifty thousand dollars and taken eighteen days." Jim drew the intersection point.

"But what would we do if we had actually spent seventy thousand dollars and taken twenty-three days for the first chunk of the project?" he asked.

Jim drew a line from the corner of the graph to the intersection point of seventy thousand dollars and twenty-three days. "We can see that our performance is way off compared to where it should be. If we allow this trend to continue, the entire project will get further and further off track. Monitoring the time and budget of each chunk allows us to identify problems and take corrective action. Remember, when you fly in an airplane it's actually off course 95 percent of the time. The pilot is continually adjusting the flight path to get you to the right destination."

Manion drew two equations on the flip chart. The first read:

COST EFFICIENCY = BUDGET/ACTUAL.

The second read:

TIME EFFICIENCY = ESTIMATED TIME/ACTUAL TIME.

"At this point our cost efficiency is fifty thousand dollars divided by seventy thousand, or 71.4 percent. Our time efficiency is eighteen days divided by twenty-three days, or 78.3 percent. Either way, we know we need to stop and regroup. Continuing on this project without any revisions to our plan will simply lead us to miss both our cost and our time targets. Be an airplane pilot with every project. Be prepared to make adjustments as you go along to keep your work on time and within budget.

"Setting measurable performance standards as well as time and cost estimates for each chunk is critical. It makes the plan into a living document we can use to manage change throughout the life of the project. If we have effectively managed each chunk, we won't have any surprises at the end of the project. That's how we get to MONITOR PROGRESS."

Manion turned off the overhead projector and took a few minutes to answer questions from the students. Then he began the final portion of his presentation. "I mentioned to you that there were two things you needed in order to be successful in managing change. We covered the first, project management. Can anyone tell me what the other thing is?"

The audience was silent. Jim smiled broadly. "People.

More specifically, the ability to work with people. Regardless of how bright you may be, or how well you may perform on an individual basis, if you can't work with other people, if you are a negative influence in the workplace, you are expendable. The days of the creative genius prima donna are over. Budgets are too tight. Performance demands are too high. And that applies to any job in any industry, not just advertising."

■

If you are a negative influence in the workplace, you are expendable.

■

Manion picked up a marker and drew a tall, narrow pyramid on the flip chart. "In the old days companies were structured vertically. There were numerous management layers that acted as filters between senior management and other levels in the organization. In those days people throughout the organization often got away with murder. They'd treat people they worked with like dirt, and as long as the job got done, management didn't care. There was enough slack in the organization to cover up the abuses and waste."

Jim then drew a wide-based, short pyramid on the flip chart. "Things have changed. Today even in the largest companies there may only be four or five levels between the CEO and the warehouse shipper. The communication channels to senior management are more direct. The filtering effects are greatly reduced. Most of the fat in organizations disappeared long ago, so companies simply cannot tolerate disruptive personalities. To be successful managers of change not only do you need to practice effective project management; you need to be good at people management as well. That means you need to be a team player. There are two things I want you to remember about dealing with people. If you follow these guidelines you cannot help but become an effective team player."

Manion walked to the overhead projector, turned it on, and read the projected text to the audience. "YOUR PERCEPTIONS CREATE YOUR RELATIONSHIPS."

He continued, "This is a concept that many of us may have trouble accepting. Sure, it's a lot easier to blame other people when you have a difficult time with them. But then you fail to address the core issue. If you focus on what's bad about another person, you will automatically react to the negative traits you are expecting to see. It will become next to impossible for you to create a workable, positive relationship with that person."

One of the students raised her hand vigorously then spoke out. "But Mr. Manion, some people are just plain miserable all the time. Are you trying to say that you can somehow change their behavior?"

Jim looked at the student with a trace of a smile on his face. The question was all too familiar. "No, I'm not trying to suggest that you can force a change in someone else's behavior. People do what they do. What I am saying is that how we interpret what others do can have a significant bearing on how we perceive them. If we choose to perceive someone in a negative light, we expect and react to their negative behaviors. We torpedo any chance for a good relationship to develop."

Manion moved closer to the student and continued, "On the other hand, if we consciously try to focus on the positive aspects of other people, we can't help but develop better relationships with them. That's because we expect and react to their positive traits. When I find myself in a difficult interaction, I remind myself that I own the emotions I feel. I create them by how I interpret the world around me.

No one makes me feel anything. It's the same for each of you."

We own the emotions we feel. We create them by how we interpret the world.

Jim extended his hand, palm up, to the student. "Look, . . . it's true that you will encounter people who are, as you put it, miserable all the time. All you can do in such cases is accept responsibility for the emotions you feel when you are around such people. It's your choice. You allow them to get to you when you internalize and personalize their behavior. You don't have to create a negative emotional reaction within yourself."

The student cocked her head to one side, took a moment to digest what Jim was saying, then nodded her head in agreement.

Manion changed the graphic on the overhead projector. "Everyone can make a contribution. Everyone can make a difference." Then he paused to collect his thoughts. Scenes from the office flashed through his brain. "If you enter every workday with this thought in mind, you will begin to see everyone you come in contact with as an untapped resource. When you take the time to ask other people for input, you will be amazed at their creativity and how much they care about what they do."

Manion clenched his fist and drove it into the palm of his other hand as he continued. "There has never been a person born who didn't want to do a good job. At some point everyone in business was just like each of you in this room—young, energetic, enthusiastic, full of dreams."

Jim slowed the pace of his delivery and lowered his

voice. "Business needs people who dare to dream and people who are willing to take a risk. That's why all of us need to remember to focus on the potential in the people around us. Once you stop believing in people, it's easy for them to stop believing in themselves. Then dreams die, the willingness to take risks dies, and ultimately organizations die."

When we stop believing in people, dreams die, risk taking dies, organizations die.

The room was silent as Manion returned to the over-head projector and switched it off. He ended his presentation by thanking the students for their time. All of them took to their feet and gave him a standing ovation. But Manion was only partially aware of their reaction. His mind was preoccupied with other thoughts.

18

WHEN JIM WALKED THROUGH HIS FRONT DOOR THAT night he could scarcely contain his energy. Karen took one glance at him and could tell that something had happened. "How did it go today at the college?" she asked.

Jim's response was rapid, the words almost tumbling over themselves as he tried to articulate what he was feeling. "It was like riding on a roller coaster. On the positive side I felt really alive and tuned in to the audience. I can't remember any business presentation that has given me such a charge. I was really into my material and the audience. On the negative side, I felt naked, like the audience was going to discover the truth about me."

Karen stepped back and looked at her husband. His gestures were accentuated. His hands were clenched into fists. His energy and excitement were tangible. She could feel it radiating from him.

"I never felt so alive. There was this indescribable sense that what I was doing was making a difference." He turned to Karen. "I actually felt like I helped to change people's lives today."

Karen was unsure of how to respond. She studied him

intently. "Why don't you tell me what happened. I'd like to understand."

Manion strode past her and down the hallway toward the kitchen. Karen followed him, hurrying to catch up as he answered her over his shoulder. "As soon as I looked out into the audience I could feel their energy. I could almost taste their anticipation. The normal fears everyone experiences prior to making a presentation dissolved. I didn't even start with the material I had prepared."

"You've never done that before."

"I know." Jim went to the kitchen sink, filled a glass with tap water, then kept talking between gulps. "It was the strangest thing. I found myself being drawn out into the audience. It was like they were a magnet."

"Well, how did you start your presentation if you didn't use your prepared material?" Karen asked.

"I just walked out among the students and started asking them questions."

Karen took a seat at the kitchen table then looked at her husband quizzically. "What kinds of questions?"

"I asked them if they were at the college and taking that particular course so they could pursue a career in advertising. Eighty percent put up their hands. Then I asked them why they wanted to work in advertising."

"What did they say?"

"Typical Hollywood movie stuff . . . the money, the glamour, the plush office." Manion pulled out the chair opposite Karen then leaned toward her, intense. "I realized that most of them were there for the wrong reasons. It wasn't the sense of excitement you feel when you're working hard on a difficult assignment. It wasn't the thrill you get when you're experiencing an idea being born. It wasn't the feeling of accomplishment that overwhelms you when your efforts get a tangible reaction from the marketplace. It was just the money and the perceived status."

"What did you expect? They aren't in the business, so how could they know about the feelings you've just described?"

"But you can have those feelings regardless of what job you do. It hit me that the students weren't different from most of the people you meet in life. People you work with. In many ways they weren't different from me. It's easy to allow yourself to get trapped in what you're doing. It's so easy to forget your dreams, to trade them for the illusion of security."

It's so easy to forget your dreams, to trade them for the illusion of security.

Rather than respond, Karen just watched Jim and waited for him to continue.

"At the end of the presentation they gave me a standing ovation, and I hardly even noticed it. Do you know why?" Jim asked.

Karen shook her head.

"I was too wrapped up in my thoughts about where *our lives* were going. I was wondering if we'd be able to make our dreams come true."

"Jim, we've got plans. We just sat down last month and talked about how we're doing with our finances."

"Sure, we sit down and talk about the budget on a regular basis. That's probably more than most couples do." Manion chuckled. "But then I realized that we really don't have an objective."

"Sure we do. We know that we want to retire and have a comfortable life in a warm climate."

Jim smiled. "That's why I felt naked during the presentation today. Here I am telling a lecture hall full of students that if they want to successfully complete a project they need to have a measurable objective, and I don't even have a plan for my own retirement. When you think about it, what does a comfortable life mean?"

"Well, to me it means not having any debts and having enough money to live comfortably," Karen replied.

"But how much is that? Thirty thousand a year? Forty thousand?" asked Manion.

"I don't know," Karen replied.

"Neither do I. The point is, unless we set a measurable target, how are we going to be able to develop a plan to get there?"

"How's anybody supposed to know?" answered Karen. "There are so many things to consider."

"As I was doing the project management part of my presentation today it hit me like a ton of bricks. If project management can make you effective at work, why not apply all the same principles to be more effective in your personal life? After all, Peter and I were just talking about using project management to work on some of my problems at work."

"So, how do you think project management would help us plan for retirement?" asked Karen.

"The first step in project management is to set a measurable objective. Let's say our goal is to be totally debt free by the time you're fifty and retire when you're sixty. That gives us our time guidelines. Then we need to set a measurable financial target. In today's terms, how much income do you think we'd need to retire to a warmer climate and have a comfortable life?" Jim asked.

"It depends what we're going to do, . . . you know, entertainment, travel." Karen looked puzzled. "I'm not sure I know where to start."

"We should begin with the end in mind," said Jim. He

grabbed a pen and some paper from a drawer in the kitchen. "Let's write down all the things we'd like to be able to do when we're retired. Where we'd like to live. What we'd like to be able to do for the children. After we have that written down, then we'll take a guess on how much after-tax income it would take to achieve that lifestyle in today's dollars."

Less than an hour later, Manion was beaming from ear to ear. "I knew it wouldn't take that long to figure out how much money we'd need."

"You're right," Karen said. "I'm surprised at how quickly we could arrive at a figure. The scary part is how big the figure is. How are we ever going to put that much money together?"

"It's like eating an elephant—one bite at a time. If we follow the next project management step, we need to break this big retirement goal into smaller pieces: reducing our debt, getting insurance coverage, saving for college for the kids, having an investment strategy, doing tax and estate planning, and so on," replied Manion. "Then we start to plan how each piece fits into the larger strategy."

"But we don't have the expertise to deal with all these issues," Karen pointed out.

"You're absolutely right. That's why we'll use the Eight Wonders of the World to help us determine what we can do ourselves and where we'll need help." Jim went on to explain the eight planning questions. Then they began to develop the outline of their retirement plan.

"I think this is about as much as we can do," Karen finally said. "We really need some professional assistance to integrate all these ideas into a formal, workable plan."

Jim nodded his head in agreement. "Why don't we both ask around the office and find out who other people use for a financial planner. Maybe we could get some recommendations. After we get the right financial planner working for us, we can put a comprehensive plan together. In project management lingo that's connecting the dots. Then we'll review the plan and try to anticipate what could go wrong and put some alternative strategies in place. That's looking for Murphy. After that it's a matter of measuring our progress and adjusting the plan as we go along."

Karen smiled broadly at her husband. "You know, just quantifying our financial goals makes me feel more in control of our future. Even if some of the goals seem out of reach at this point, at least we know what we're shooting for."

"There are lots of other areas where you can apply project management," Jim said. "I've got an employee who was really upset because he didn't get promoted last month. With project management I can help him look at his career objectively and identify some of the things he needs to do to get ready for when the next opportunity comes."

Karen nodded her head in agreement. "I can see how I could use this approach to plan a party or a vacation, make a major purchase, or help put a field trip together for Jennifer's class at school. It's obvious how I could use it to prepare for court. I bet if we worked at it, it could become a natural way of thinking about how to get things done."

"It's funny, I've used these techniques every day at work, but I never thought about applying them at home. It makes sense that whenever you're dealing with change you can use project management. For simple, small projects you don't have to write a complicated plan. But by using project management concepts, like checking to see if you have a measurable objective, you can increase your effectiveness because you're clear about what you're trying to achieve," Manion said.

"So what other pearls of wisdom did you give the students that you should be sharing at home?" asked Karen.

"There was one other thing that happened. At the end of

my presentation I was sharing some perspectives about people and the importance of teamwork. I told the students
that once you stop believing in people, it's easy for them to
stop believing in themselves."

She cocked her head to one side. Those were unusual
words from her husband. "Where did that come from, Jim?
Were you thinking about the children or something?"

"No, I wasn't thinking about the kids. At least not then.
I don't know, maybe a seed was planted with some phone
calls I made earlier this month."

"You never mentioned them."

"No, I wasn't sure what I was going to do about them. I
guess I'm still not sure. I spoke to some of the regional sales
managers who had helped me out with my presentation to
the board, and I confirmed that at least three of them had
given me information about some major sales that they
didn't pass along to Ted. One of the guys, Jacobsen, really
got a strip torn off him by Wilkinson."

"Why was Ted so upset at him?"

"Jacobsen's one of our best field people, also one of the
ones who's been with us the longest. I guess Wilkinson was
furious that his best performer would circumvent him and
talk to me instead. The guy did go against protocol: Wilkinson is his boss. He should have given him the sales information."

"Why would he do that if he knew it would get Wilkinson riled up?" asked Karen.

"From what Jacobsen told me, Ted's been very abusive
with the field staff for a couple of years now. I guess they've
been beat on for so long that most of them have lost confi-
dence that they can do anything. As I said, Jacobsen's one of
our top performers. He wouldn't have a problem getting a
job elsewhere. I guess he'd just had enough."

Manion shook his head and looked at Karen. "I talked
to Peter about this very thing after the board meeting. He

warned me that there was something going on in the sales department and to be careful about getting drawn into it."

"You don't have to get involved."

"Yeah, I suppose there are not many things that any of us really have to do." Jim looked into his wife's eyes. "But how can you not, when you know people are being mistreated? Besides, it's too late now anyway."

"What do you mean?"

"I already went to see Fontaine about it."

"How will that make you look with Fisher? You're supposed to be trying to improve your relationships at work, especially with the rest of the senior team."

"I asked Fontaine to keep our conversation completely confidential. Fisher probably won't even find out."

"And if she does?"

"Then what happens will happen. These guys took a big risk trying to help me. I can't just abandon them. I'm following up on a piece of advice Peter gave me."

"What was that?"

"He said you can only help people who are willing to help themselves. I figure these guys are."

19

SEVERAL WEEKS HAD PASSED SINCE JIM MANION'S PRE-sentation at the college. He was starting to feel comfortable at the office again. So comfortable that some of the new stresses felt just like the old ones.

Manion viewed the e-mail screen on his computer. His temper flared. "That miserable SOB hasn't even opened the mail I sent him almost ten days ago. He knows I've got a deadline to meet."

Jim picked up the telephone and quickly jabbed at four buttons. "Ted, it's Jim. I know you've been busy lately, but I really need to talk to you about a few pressing projects."

Jim could feel Ted smirking on the other end of the line as Ted responded, "Oh, Jim, sorry I haven't gotten back to you. It has been a real zoo around here lately. Can we make it next week?"

"Not really. Look, we've got some deadlines looming, and I need your input on a few issues."

"Yeah, I know. We're all running hard these days."

"Ted, it's got nothing to do with just running hard. We've got some consumer research planned to launch early next month, and we've got a dealer satisfaction survey that has to go to the mailing house within a few days. I hate to impose, but I need to see you today. Next week just won't cut it."

"Come on, Manion, are you just crying wolf again?"

Jim could feel his anger rising another notch. He paused for a few moments to try to regain his composure. "Why don't I drop over in a couple of minutes. I'll bring you a coffee. Come on, Ted, it won't even take twenty minutes to handle things."

Manion's offer was met with silence on the other end of the line. Then Wilkinson finally spoke: "OK Jim, make it a coffee and a Danish and you've got a deal. Make it a cherry Danish."

Jim clenched his teeth. "See you in a couple of minutes, Ted." He took his wallet from his suit jacket and headed off to the cafeteria. A few minutes later he arrived at Wilkinson's office carrying a small cardboard tray. Jim handed Ted a coffee and Danish, then opened the lid on his own cup.

"I brought the two surveys I need your input on, Ted."

"And good afternoon to you too, Jim."

Manion glared at Wilkinson. He paused and forced a slight smile. "Good afternoon, Ted. Look, I'm sorry I was a little abrupt today. I know you've got a hectic schedule."

"That's alright, Jim. How can I help you?"

"I need you to approve the final draft of the consumer research questionnaire we're scheduled to send out early next month. It's a large study—over five thousand pieces are going to be mailed. I want to do one final double check to make sure we've covered all the important topics," Manion said.

"What kind of response rate are you expecting?" asked Wilkinson.

"Twenty percent."

"That's all? Twenty percent of five thousand will only give you a sample size of a thousand. Is that big enough to be accurate?"

"Ted, we've already been over the sample size and methodology in previous meetings. Yes, the sample size will give us the mathematical accuracy we're looking for," Manion responded. Ted was acting true to form, trying to rehash issues that had already been addressed by the management team and make it look as if Manion didn't know what he was doing.

"Just checking. You know how some of these little details can get overlooked sometimes." Ted scanned the questionnaire, feigning interest. "This is going out early next month?"

"Uh-huh. It's scheduled for the fifth. It has to go out on that day or we risk not getting data back in time to launch the advertising campaign to support upcoming major consumer shows."

"I see." Wilkinson continued to examine the document. "Look Jim, there's just a few points, here in questions five, eight, and twelve. I don't want to make unilateral changes without getting some feedback from some of my key field people."

Ted looked up and smiled at Manion. "If I promise to get it back to you on Thursday, could I have two extra days to get some field input? It will ensure that these key questions are relevant. You do want the best possible research, don't you?"

Jim studied Wilkinson for a few moments. "Of course we want the best research we can get, Ted. But if the information isn't timely, it isn't worth doing at all. Look, if we absolutely have to, we can push the research house to the wall and give them the final draft on Thursday. But that's it, Ted. We'll probably incur some overtime charges pushing it that far."

"No problem. I'll have this final research draft back to you first thing Thursday morning." Ted turned around casually and placed the document on the credenza behind his desk. "That's the first item handled. What else can I do for you Jim? Are you going to give me the real deadline up front on this one?"

"What do you mean 'the real deadline up front'?" Manion's voice carried an abrasive edge.

"Hey, no need to get caustic with me," Wilkinson shot back. "It was you who came in here telling me that research draft had to be approved today, and then you admitted Thursday will do. I'm just trying to manage my time around real priorities."

"I explained that if we wait till Thursday we'll incur overtime charges if . . . Never mind." The frustration in Manion's voice increased. "Let's make this other item really simple. I need your feedback on this dealer satisfaction study this afternoon, before I leave your office, or it goes the way it is. Can you handle that?"

"My, my . . . we are a little testy today." Ted extended his right hand and gestured for Manion to give him the papers. "I'll humor you, Jim. But I don't know why I put out the effort. You'll end up doing what you want to do anyway."

Ted sighed deeply and rotated his chair ninety degrees so he was at a right angle to the chair Manion was sitting in. He kept his gaze focused on the survey as he continued speaking. "Jim, you know what your problem is? You're always trying to make the projects you work on into a big deal. You should lighten up a little and take yourself a little less seriously."

Ted's eyes darted at Manion to gauge his reaction. "You know, Jim, it's pretty important around here to make a good impression with the queen bee in the corner office."

Wilkinson flipped a survey page. "It sounds like things haven't been going too well for you lately." He flipped another page, trying to act casual.

"What's that supposed to mean?" Jim asked.

Wilkinson's head rolled slowly to one side. He smiled at Jim. "Oh, you know . . . silly office talk." Ted turned his attention back to the survey. "I'm sure it's probably nothing to worry about."

Jim felt trapped. The conversation was agonizing. He decided to press for a decision on the survey. "Ted, I don't want to take too much of your time. How does the questionnaire look?"

Wilkinson handed it back to Manion. "It looks fine to me. Do you need me to sign off on it or anything?"

"No, that's OK."

Ted smiled at Manion. "You should let Donato have one last look at it too. I find she makes interesting comments on all sorts of topics."

Manion glared at Wilkinson. He wanted to vault over the desk and grab Wilkinson by the collar. Instead, he picked up the questionnaire and made an abrupt exit without saying a word. As he entered the hall and turned toward his office Manion heard Wilkinson call out, "You're welcome."

20

Manion's car screeched to a halt in his driveway. He grabbed his jacket and briefcase and flung open the car door. It snapped back on its hinges and banged his left shin. Jim winced, then pounded the door panel with his fist, cursing under his breath. He held the door open with his left arm as he exited. After locking the door he looked up to see Jennifer running out of the house to greet him.

"Hi sweetie." Jim greeted her in a monotone voice. He bent down to give his daughter a kiss as she hugged him.

"Hi Daddy. You know what? I went to Brenda's house after school today and we played games. Brenda's mom let us use some of her jewelry. She had earrings and necklaces. There was one made of red beads that I really liked. Then we played a new game she got for her birthday. It was really neat. We played . . . "

Manion looked down at his daughter. His voice softened. "Maybe you could tell me about it later, OK? Daddy's pretty tired tonight."

The disappointment was etched in Jennifer's face as she replied, "That's OK. I can tell you later."

Jim followed her into the house. After closing the front door he turned to open the closet and almost tripped over a basketball Bryan had left in the entrance hall. The muscles in his jaw twitched as he kicked the basketball, sending it airborne into the living room.

He yelled out to his son, "Bryan, how many times do I have to tell you to put your things away? If you can't look after this junk, maybe I should pitch it out."

Bryan appeared from around the corner. "Sorry Dad . . . I'll put my stuff away."

"Sorry. Sorry. That's all I hear from you kids. . . . "

Karen appeared in the hallway behind her husband. She raised her eyebrows and shrugged her shoulders at the children. Then with a slight nod of her head, she motioned for them to go upstairs.

"Nice to see you home a little earlier than usual. Sounds like you had a rough day."

Jim turned away from Karen, took off his tie, and tossed it, along with his jacket, onto the railing leading upstairs. "Just when you think things are going well, Wham!" The sound of his fist smacking into his palm echoed through the hallway. "I guess it just goes to show you can't trust anyone."

Karen had seldom seen him so angry. A furrow developed in her brow. "What the heck happened today?" she asked.

"Wilkinson is what happened today. The SOB has been purposely avoiding me the past two or three weeks. It's virtually impossible to get him to cooperate on anything. All he does is needle and prod me."

"Why don't you just ignore him?"

Manion looked at his wife with disdain. "Ignore him. Well that's a super piece of advice! How many university courses did it take to come up with that one?"

"Jim, that's not fair."

"Life's like that. Welcome to the real world."

Karen turned and walked into the living room. She picked up the basketball and tossed it to Manion.

"I don't want to play catch," he said.

"Neither do we," replied Karen. "Stop throwing your emotions around at us."

The fire burning in Karen's eyes immobilized Manion. He became aware of the pulse throbbing in his head. He felt the rocklike tightness in his jaw. He saw the white knuckles of his clenched fists.

Manion closed his eyes and forced a picture of Wilkinson into his brain. "I'm sorry. It's that damn Ted. I tried all I could today to cooperate with him. He just kept goading me. Throwing cheap insults. He knows things can't get done without his input, and he taunts me with it."

Jim opened his eyes and looked at Karen. The softness in her face had returned. "I almost totally lost it today. I wanted to leap across his desk and grab him by the throat. It scared me."

"Let's go for a walk. The fresh air will do us both some good."

Karen went to the stairs and called up to the children, "Dad and I are going for a walk. Everything's fine. Order in a pizza for dinner. The phone number is on the bulletin board, and there's some money on the kitchen counter. We'll be back in a few minutes."

Karen followed Jim out the door. She took his hand as they walked down the driveway.

"We'll walk, and you talk when you're ready, OK?"

Jim stared at the pavement as they walked, barely turning his head when he looked at Karen. "Thanks. I'm OK."

The couple strolled through the neighborhood for fifteen minutes before Jim could open up, Karen with her elbow hooked behind Jim's arm so she could be closer to him. Finally he started to give her a detailed account of his altercation with Ted Wilkinson.

"I guess what really set me off was Wilkinson hinting that he knew my job was on the line," said Manion. "He was really sly about it. Like the whole world knew, and I was the only idiot who didn't."

"That's not possible. How could Wilkinson know anything?"

"I don't know. Then at the end of the conversation he drops this huge hint that he's been talking about me with Lynne Donato. That's when I really saw red." Jim shook his head in disgust. "I've been working so closely with her for the last few weeks. I thought I really had an ally. Then I find out she's talking about me behind my back. If I hadn't left the room at that point, I swear I would have strangled him."

"It's only Ted's word. You don't know for sure that Lynne talked to him about your job situation."

"It doesn't make any sense. Why would he say he had talked to her about it if he hadn't? It's not like I can't verify the facts," said Jim.

"But think about it for a minute. How many people would dare to check on something like that? You'd have to walk up to Lynne and ask her point-blank if she's been talking about you behind your back. It would take a lot of guts on your part to approach her. And then, even if you asked the question, would you expect her to admit to what she'd done? If she's like most people, she'd probably deny it."

"If I asked her, I'm sure I could tell whether she was lying to me. People can't recover that quickly when a question like that comes at them out of left field," Manion replied.

"Well, you have part of your solution then. Can you do it?" asked Karen.

Jim thought for a few minutes. "I'll do it tomorrow. Lynne and I have a project team meeting in the morning. After the rest of the group clears out of the boardroom I'll put the question to her."

"Good. At least you'll know what side of the fence Lynne is sitting on. How are you going to deal with Wilkinson?"

Manion shook his head. "After what happened today, I don't know. I'm sure he took great pleasure in getting me going. God only knows what he'll have up his sleeve tomorrow."

"I haven't seen you do your breathing exercises for a while. I've missed poking you in the gut."

Jim chuckled. "Gee, and the bruises were just disappearing. You're right, though, I haven't had the time to do any of the exercises Peter gave me for over a couple of weeks."

"You haven't had the time, or you haven't made the time?" asked Karen.

"Haven't made the time," Manion answered. "I walked into Ted's office looking for a confrontation, and I got one."

"Well, that tells you that you need to get back into the exercises Peter gave you. Maybe you should pay him a little visit for a refresher course." She gave Jim's hand a squeeze for emphasis.

Manion nodded his agreement. "Let's go home. The pizza's probably getting cold."

21

As he entered the pub, Manion scanned the tables for a moment before he saw Peter Miller waving to him from a table in the corner. He walked over, smiling. The men shook hands warmly.

"This is a rare privilege," said Miller. "I can't remember the last time I got you out to a pub."

"It's been a while. What are you drinking?"

"Newcastle."

Jim called out to one of the waitresses, "Two mugs of Newcastle, big ones."

"Big ones?" mused Peter. "Either this is a big party, or it's a big problem." Miller looked at his friend closely. "Not hard to tell. What's wrong?"

Jim got right to the point. "Things at work were going just as we planned until the last week or so. Lately people seem to be so uptight. Wilkinson's been a bigger jackass than usual. It was all I could do not to throttle him yesterday."

"What's he been up to?" asked Peter.

"He's been more uncooperative than ever. It's next to impossible to get him to work with me on anything. He tries to trip me up every chance he gets."

174

"Well Jim, that's perfectly understandable. The board meeting wasn't that long ago. Wilkinson still has to be feeling very vulnerable knowing that some of his field guys have been leaving him out of the loop and talking to you."

"I tried to help him at the board meeting. It would have been easier to make him look bad."

"That's what's making him paranoid, Jim. He knows what you could have done to him but didn't. Now he's wondering whether you'll change your mind when the next opportunity arises."

"The SOB should be worried. Considering how he's been baiting me and trying to set me up, I should nail him to the wall." Jim took a gulp from his mug.

"So what set you off yesterday?" asked Miller.

"I needed to get Ted's input on a couple of research projects. He's been avoiding them totally. He hasn't read any of the e-mail messages I've sent him for a week and a half. Time was getting tight on both projects, so I had to force the issue with him. I had to bribe him with coffee and a Danish just to get twenty minutes of his time."

"You bought him coffee and a Danish?!" Peter laughed out loud. "With what you've told me about his personality, that's like giving a junkie free heroin. Wilkinson feeds on being in control."

Manion scowled. "Hey, I don't have your professional training. I make mistakes."

"No argument from me on that point."

"Why didn't you warn me?"

Miller smiled. "Some things you only learn by doing."

"Thanks a lot. Anyway, I went over to see him." He stopped and looked at Peter. "Wrong office, right?"

Peter looked pensive. "Possibly."

"I tried to push Ted for some decisions I needed on the questionnaires. He kept changing the subject . . . talking about details that we'd already discussed months ago—anything but give me what I needed. I got really frustrated and got a little abrasive with him."

Miller interrupted. "And he twisted that little bit of abrasiveness around to make it seem like you were the antagonist."

Manion's head snapped back in surprise. "You really do know his type. Alright, smart guy, so what happened next?"

"My guess would be that he just kept turning up the subtle pressure on you, trying to make you lose control. A series of little digs and jabs, innuendos," Miller said.

"Bull's-eye."

"What was his coupe de grâce?" asked Peter.

"Toward the end of the meeting he said he'd heard talk around the office that I was in trouble with Fisher. Then he implied that Lynne Donato had been talking to him about me losing my job. It was a double whammy."

Miller applauded quietly and quipped, "He's very skillful. Was there any truth to the story about Donato?"

"Last night Karen suggested that I talk to Lynne, so today I asked her straight out if she and Ted had talked about my job being on the line. She admitted that a conversation had occurred, but she said that it was Ted who had brought up the subject. Her opinion was that Ted was testing a theory of his before he put it out on the rumor mill."

"Do you believe her?"

"One hundred percent."

"Why?"

"Because she went on to say that she had told Fontaine about her conversation with Ted, although she didn't mention Ted by name, and that she asked Philippe for advice. Apparently Fontaine went back to Fisher about it. Eventually they asked Lynne to try to kill the rumor before it got out by confronting Ted about it. The way she described it, I had to believe her."

"That's great. At least you know that Lynne is definitely

in your camp. It's nice to be able to count on her support. It's also important to know that Fisher and Fontaine worked with Donato to try to kill Ted's rumor. That proves that they're trying to give you a fair shot at turning yourself around," Peter observed.

Miller gulped down some more ale. "Having people in your corner helps, but it still doesn't solve the problem of the skillful Mr. Wilkinson."

"That's the problem, Peter. He's got me off balance because I'm not sure what he's going to do next. I avoided him all day today."

Peter shook his head. "Can't do that, Jim. That gives him the control he wants. You play right into his hands. You can't afford to let him get you on the run. Besides, he's a key member of the management team. You have to find ways of working with him effectively. How did you prepare for the meeting with him yesterday?"

"What do you mean?"

"Mental rehearsal . . . what did you use?" Miller asked.

"I didn't use anything."

Peter's eyes narrowed. "What do you mean you didn't use anything? We went over all this stuff a month and a half ago."

"I've been pretty busy. . . . "

Miller crossed his arms over his chest and stared at his friend. "When did you stop using the techniques I showed you?"

"I don't know, a couple of weeks ago maybe."

"You've only got five or six weeks left before they're going to make a decision about you."

"I know that."

"Then why would you stop using the techniques I showed you—the relaxation exercise, the visualizations, the affirmations, the mental rehearsals?"

Manion looked down at the table and shook his head. "I

don't know. I was doing everything just like we discussed, and it was starting to work. Things were beginning to go really well. I was getting along better with people at work. I was feeling a lot more comfortable." Jim looked up at Miller. "I guess I thought that since everything was starting to turn around, I could slack off a little. Slacking off turned into stopping."

Miller motioned to one of the waitresses. "Can I get a paper cup and a knife?" he asked.

The waitress wrinkled her nose. "What for?"

"A scientific experiment."

"Sure, just give me a minute or two."

Peter turned to Manion. "Drink your beer, but don't let her have your glass."

In a few moments the waitress returned with the paper cup and knife Miller had requested. Peter took them from her and began using the knife to punch holes in the bottom of the paper cup.

"You're a visual learner, Jim. I want you to watch carefully so you'll always remember this concept."

Miller held up the paper cup. "This is a person. You. Me. Anyone. When we act in negative ways, it's because we're empty on the inside, just like this cup. Our feelings of self-worth, self-esteem are low. So we try to fill the void by attacking other people, somehow taking esteem from them. The emptier we are, the more prone we are to attacking others."

When we're empty on the inside, we try to fill the void by attacking other people.

"Makes sense."

"If you use the affirmations and visualizations properly,

you can fill the void without having to take something away from somebody else."

Peter held the paper cup over Manion's empty beer mug and began pouring his own beer into the paper cup. As Miller poured the beer it began to leak out of the holes he had punched in the bottom of the paper cup.

"The affirmations and visualizations are like the beer filling the empty paper cup. We use the techniques to build up our self-esteem and self-image. You filled the emptiness, and that's why things started to go better for you at work. As you filled up your cup, the need to attack and take from others was gradually eliminated," Peter explained.

Manion watched as the liquid drained from the paper cup into his once-empty beer mug.

"Jim, none of us has a perfect container to pour our supply of self-esteem into. Because of all the negative influences around us, it's natural for some of the positive stuff to leak out. When you stop using the visualizations and the affirmations, eventually the positive effects disappear. You're left with an empty cup again. That's when you revert back to your old behavior."

"So if I want to change my performance and behavior in the long term, I have to use the techniques continuously."

"Absolutely, every day that goes by without reinforcement depletes your supply of self-esteem and weakens your self-image. Once your self-image starts to erode, the positive perceptions of the world you've been trying to maintain erode as well. Before you know it you're back on the downside of the performance spiral."

Jim nodded his head in agreement. "I've been there before, and I don't want to go there again."

Miller reached across the table and put his hand on Manion's shoulder. "Jim, you've already started on the way down again. Your behavior should tell you that. The change in your perceptions of the people around you should tell you that. The only person who is in charge of your life is you.

We can have as many meetings like this as you want, but ultimately you have to be prepared to fill the cup. No one else can do it for you."

Ultimately you have to be prepared to fill your cup. No one else can do it for you.

"I know."

"Jim, you've still got time to fill the cup again. It's been leaking for the past couple of weeks, but it's not empty. If it were, you wouldn't have been able to exercise the amount of self-control you did with Wilkinson. You've got maybe six weeks left until D-Day with Fisher. Forty-two days to develop a habit that will keep you filling your cup for a lifetime.

"This isn't a game. It's your life. One thing is certain: you're going to have to start, right away, to work on a few visualizations and affirmations about how you'd like to deal with Wilkinson. We have to get a new reaction programmed into you so he won't be able to pull your chain.

"Whenever you allow him to get to you and create a negative emotion, he has control over you," said Peter. "Remember, it's not his emotion, it's yours. You created it within you. You own it."

Manion shook his head. "I feel like such a hypocrite."

"Why?"

"A couple of weeks ago I stood up in front of a group of students at the college and told them the same thing, and now I find myself not even practicing what I've been preaching."

"Jim, we all catch ourselves in those situations. None of us is perfect. That's why it's critical to keep monitoring your perceptions. Remember the envelope exercises we did?"

"Sure."

"There's no reason you can't do the same thing at any time during the day. It's a great way to check where your thinking is at the moment. You have to establish your starting point if you want to change what's going on in your head."

"Just like the first step in project management. Set a measurable objective: from where to where by when," said Manion.

"Absolutely. Changing your thought patterns is still change. To effectively implement change you still need to manage it. You have to know where you are now and where you want to get to in the future. The techniques I shared with you earlier—relaxation, affirmations, visualizations, and mental rehearsals—are the tools you need to use to make changes in your thought patterns.

"Before going into a meeting with someone, quickly jot down adjectives to describe the person. That will identify what perceptions you are working with. It's like early-warning radar. . . . It will tell you what kind of meeting you're likely to have. If you don't like the prognosis, then you'll need to change your perceptions and the behavior they produce before you get into the meeting. The only way to do that effectively is through the four tools."

Jim interrupted Miller. "Relaxation, affirmations, visualizations, and mental rehearsal."

Miller smiled. "I love a good student. Remember when we talked about freeze-frame?"

"That's when we lock on to a particular perception of someone or something, either good or bad."

"That's right. Now, if the adjectives you jot down indicate you're going into a meeting with a very negative view of someone, you have to stop and refocus on something positive about that person, or at the very least neutral. Then build on that new, more positive freeze-frame with your visualization, affirmation, and mental rehearsal techniques. Let's start working on your next encounter with your artful associate."

"Yeah, right. It's not like I'm feeling warm and fuzzy about Ted at the moment."

"Then this is the perfect time to test your ability to re-focus," said Peter.

"Something positive about Wilkinson . . . you're not asking for too much!" Jim let his gaze drift around the pub as he thought for a moment. "OK, the guy can sell."

"That's the best you can do? The guy can sell?"

"Alright, I'll admit it, he's terrific with customers. I've seen him wrangle the company out of some pretty tight situations and close some deals I thought were impossible."

"I imagine those situations are highly stressful for him."

"Sure."

"And I suppose his job takes a lot of diplomacy."

"At times."

"Well, let's assume that Ted uses up his natural quota of diplomacy on customers and doesn't have much left over for you, and that's why he acts a little erratic. So it's not purposeful on his part. His supply of diplomacy is simply tapped out. How could you use that scenario to establish a new focus and build a new response to him using the tools we talked about?"

"I forget where to start."

"WIPE," said Peter, removing a pen from his jacket pocket and handing it to Jim with a paper napkin.

"WIPE. Write an affirmation to wipe out my old behavior. I have to focus on what I want to have happen, use the pronoun *I* to make it personal, keep it in the present tense, and add a positive emotion."

"So write your affirmation, sport," said Peter, signalling the waitress for another round of beers.

Jim worked on his statement for a couple of minutes then pushed the napkin in front of Peter when he'd finished.

Peter read the statement aloud: "I feel terrific when I ignore Ted's digs and remain calm and composed when I deal with him." Then he began to test the affirmation. "OK, let's check it out. Have you focused on what you want to have happen?"

"Sure, ignore the digs and remain calm and composed," Jim answered.

"Check one."

"It's personal and I've kept it in the present tense."

"Check two and three."

"And by saying that I feel terrific, I've built in a positive emotion."

"Check four. What visualization goes with it?"

Jim's eyes darted up and to the right. "We're in Ted's office and he starts to get testy. . . . "

"Be more specific."

"He starts to rehash old information and second-guess decisions to try to get me going."

"What do you see yourself doing?"

"I simply answer his questions objectively and keep guiding the conversation back to the subject I came to discuss."

"You have to make the visualization as real as possible. You need to hear the conversation in your mind. You need to see the body language. You have to feel like you're there."

"I can get it pretty clear."

"Good. How are you feeling in your mental picture?"

"Patient."

"Why?"

"Ted's had a tough day with customers, and he's just trying to let off some steam at me because I'm a safe target."

"That's a good start, Jim. You have to observe Wilkinson every chance you get so you can build as much reality into your visualization as possible. Watch him with other people and be very conscious of his behavior patterns. Monitor what sets him off and what calms him down."

"Alright."

"Now what mental rehearsals would you use?"

"Wouldn't I just use the same visualization over and over?"

"OK, if that's the most likely scenario. But you should also try to think about other specific situations in which you have allowed Ted to get to you. Replay those in your mind, but visualize yourself behaving in a calm and composed manner. You can use the same affirmation for a range of different scenes."

"So if another likely situation comes up I'll still be able to handle it."

"That's right. If you rehearse enough times mentally, when those real-life situations crop up again, you'll react to them with the new program—calm and composed," said Peter. "You've already learned that going onto Wilkinson's turf without being prepared is suicide. There's no excuse now, you've got the tools."

22

A MONTH HAD PASSED SINCE JIM MANION'S MEETING with Peter Miller in the pub. Manion had been religious about doing his daily relaxation exercises, followed by affirmations, visualizations, and mental rehearsals. His progress was the topic of conversation.

Katherine looked up as Philippe tapped on her door. "Come in, Philippe, it's good to see you. My travel schedule has been so brutal the past six weeks I've hardly even been in the office. . . . It must be almost a month since we've actually sat down together."

"It's been a while."

"You said you had a couple of things you wanted to review this morning."

"The first thing I thought we could do is go over Jim Manion's file. We started this two and a half months ago. We're scheduled to make a decision about him within the next few weeks."

Fisher smiled at Philippe. "That should be an easy one."

"I thought that's how you'd feel."

"Thanks for keeping me abreast of his progress with your weekly status reports. They've really helped me keep in touch when I've been on the road," said Katherine.

Fontaine opened a file folder as he sat down at the conference table in her office. "Jim and I have been meeting regularly, so the updates were easy to do."

"He seems to be getting along much better with most of the senior team. The board meeting seems to have been the turning point. Your reports indicate that even though he's had a couple of minor glitches over the past six weeks, he has been making steady progress."

"Definitely. There have been a couple of skirmishes with Ted, but that's to be expected given the earlier concern we had about the rumor mill," replied Philippe.

"I see the employee involvement program has been really active lately."

"The team has been working a lot more creatively since Jim joined a little over a month ago. He put us through one of his project management sessions."

"I bet the first thing out of his mouth was 'What's the objective?'" said Katherine.

"That's Jim alright. But that one question really helped us realize that we didn't have a quantifiable objective for the team. After some discussion we decided it was important to create a range of opportunities so that everyone could get involved if they wanted to."

"Is that where the idea for cross-functional product launch teams came from?"

"Yes."

"I understand that you're setting up three of them to work on launching our new products."

"That's right, each team has members from marketing, sales, manufacturing, engineering, finance, distribution, and human resources. Their objective is to develop a detailed internal launch plan and budget for their assigned product. Since many of the team members haven't worked on this type of assignment before, my department developed a selection process and training plan for each team member. Thanks for approving the budget for the behavior profiling software I requested. We've done behavior assessments on most of the team members."

"How's that software program from Carlson Learning Company working out?"

"Everybody seems comfortable with the Personal Profile System. It's easy to administer, and the software makes scoring a breeze. The team members seem impressed that we'd make that kind of investment to try to encourage a good team environment. It gives the managers a good look at their own behavior and gives their employees a chance to look at themselves as well, which makes it easier for me to coach them on improving their interpersonal skills.

"After the behavior assessments, we've been conducting in-depth training to help team members learn how to identify basic behavior styles in themselves and others. Then we teach them how to be more effective in dealing with the potential conflicts that arise between the different behavior styles. If individuals want to share their personal results with other members of their department or team, they're free to do so, but we're keeping it on a voluntary basis. We want to make sure everyone stays comfortable with what we're doing."

"Good. What about the rest of the training plans?"

"Those are under way. Jim's volunteered to be one of the coaches for a test program."

"On project management?"

"No, personal management skills."

Katherine looked confused. "Personal management skills? I must have missed something. What's that all about?"

"They're skills designed to help people change their attitudes and self-image. Jim's been using them extensively in his own turnaround. The program involves a combination of relaxation and visualization exercises, along with some structured statements called affirmations. Jim really pushed me to add the material to the training curriculum."

"You're sure about this, Philippe?"

"I was a little skeptical at first, but the change in Jim has been so positive it prompted me to do some investigating. I found out that a number of Fortune 500 companies are using the same techniques with some success. They're particularly useful when your organization is going through a period of significant change, and ingrained employee attitudes are causing resistance. We're going to start using the techniques on a very limited basis and see what happens."

"Sounds interesting. Make sure you keep me updated on the effects. Maybe it's something we can roll out to the entire staff?"

"So you're pleased with Jim's progress to this point?"

"Yes, it looks like he's well on his way. What else did you want to discuss?"

Philippe removed a form from his file folder and placed it in front of Katherine. "This is the other issue I want to discuss. It's a transfer approval request for Jacobsen."

Fisher picked up the paper, scanned it quickly, then looked up at Philippe with surprise. "He's been working on the West Coast the whole time he's been with us. That's almost twenty years. I assumed he wanted to stay out there. . . . Most folks from the West Coast do."

"I don't want you to approve the request, Katherine," replied Fontaine.

"Jacobsen's been one of our top regional sales managers every year. If he wants to move to the south central region, I'm not going to stand in his way," Fisher responded.

"This may sound like I'm changing subjects, so bear with me. Do you remember the board meeting when Wilkinson was being grilled about those three seasonal accounts?" asked Fontaine.

"Sure," replied Fisher. "It was almost an unbelievable coincidence that they had all placed large orders just before the meeting." Katherine smiled broadly. "I guess once in a while fate works on your side."

Philippe looked her in the eye, his face expressionless. "Ted didn't have a clue about those orders."

"He just forgot about them. Remember, . . . Ted told Manion over coffee," said Katherine.

"Manion made that up."

"How do you know that?"

"Jim told me almost six weeks ago."

"Why didn't you mention it earlier?"

"I wasn't sure there was a reason to."

"Why mention it now?"

Fontaine looked at the transfer request in Katherine's hand. "You're holding the reason."

Fisher looked at the transfer approval request, then back at Philippe. "You'd better explain."

"Jim gave me a call over a month ago and said that something unusual had happened when he was preparing for that board meeting. He explained that he had been in contact with some of the regional sales managers so he could get input on his new product launches. During those conversations Jim had asked the salespeople to keep him informed of any late-breaking sales. He told them the information could be crucial to the outcome of the board meeting."

"It certainly was," noted Fisher.

"Well, some of the salespeople took Manion's request seriously, because four or five of them called him just before the board meeting with details on some new orders. Jim went into the meeting assuming that Ted also had that information. Remember when Wilkinson hit that rough spot in the board meeting? Manion volunteered the information to the board but gave Ted credit for it," explained Fontaine.

Katherine looked straight at Philippe, her attention focused on every word he was saying.

"You may remember that Ted was a little abrupt at the end of the meeting. Manion didn't think anything of it. After all, their relationship has never been very good. Later that day Jim made some follow-up calls to the regional folks who had given him the sales updates. He wanted to thank them for their efforts. It was during those calls that he discovered that at least three of our regional people had never told Wilkinson about the late-breaking deals."

Fisher's eyes narrowed. "They told Manion but not Wilkinson?"

"Exactly. Jim thought that was very unusual, and he wanted me to know about it."

"Did he say anything else? Did he give you any reasons why he thought the salespeople would give him the information but keep it from Ted?"

"Yes. He told me that some of the regional sales managers were very frustrated with Ted, that they accused him of being very abusive with them. Jim felt an obligation to pass their feelings on to me, and he was also very concerned that his turnaround would be compromised if we thought that he was fabricating this story about Ted to deflect attention away from himself. He asked me not to discuss it with you unless it became a substantive issue."

"I can understand why he would feel that way. Did he tell you who the salespeople were?" asked Katherine.

"Yes, he did." Fontaine looked at the transfer approval request.

"Jacobsen was one of them?" Fisher was astonished.

Fontaine nodded his head in agreement. "Wilkinson called me before he sent the transfer approval form through. He told me that Jacobsen had another job offer for big dollars. He said the only chance we had to keep Jacobsen was to move him into a more lucrative territory."

"South central." Katherine's mind was racing.

"Ted asked me to pull out all the stops to get the transfer approved quickly." Philippe twirled his pencil around and tapped the table several times with the eraser end. "I wouldn't have thought much about Ted's request if it hadn't been for the conversation I'd had with Manion. Something just didn't feel right."

"It smells a little funny, doesn't it?" replied Fisher. "What did you do next?"

"I called Jacobsen and asked him to level with me about his plans for the future."

"And?"

"And Jacobsen said he didn't know anything about a transfer. The issue had never been discussed. He admitted that he had received a couple of offers, which he was seriously considering. But here's the kicker: I asked him about the money, and he told me that money had nothing to do with it. He also told me that he'd quit before he'd accept a transfer to the south central region."

Katherine's mind leapt ahead. "It's Wilkinson. Jacobsen's got problems with Ted."

"Big time," replied Philippe. "From what Jacobsen told me, a lot of the other folks do as well. They're afraid to say anything. But it looks like Jacobsen's past the point of caring what Wilkinson might do to him."

"How much of this do you think is just smoke?" asked Fisher.

"At this stage there's no way of telling without digging into it. Once we open up this can of worms, we'd better be prepared to empty it," said Fontaine.

Katherine placed the transfer approval request on the table and tapped it lightly with the palm of her hand. "Obviously this needs to stay put for a while until we're sure we know what's really going on. Why don't you tell Wilkinson that I wouldn't approve the transfer for budget reasons, that I want to wait for the next quarterly results. Call the other two regional sales managers who gave Manion information but kept it from Wilkinson."

"My gut tells me that they'll support Jacobsen's view," said Fontaine.

"Philippe, if things start looking worse, keep digging until you have a complete picture. If you find there's a serious problem with our sales management, I need you to come up with some options for how to deal with it."

23

KAREN FINISHED WITH A FILE AND PLACED IT IN HER OUT tray. Her mind had been wandering since she arrived at the office that morning. Every couple of minutes she'd glance down at her wristwatch to check the time.

"It's nine-forty-five," she thought. "I wonder if Jim is out of his meeting yet."

Karen bit her lower lip then looked at the telephone and contemplated calling his office. Her palms grew damp. "No," she thought. "Jim said he'd call when he got out of Fontaine's office."

Things had been going much better at work for Jim the past month and a half since his last meeting with Peter Miller. He was coping better with Wilkinson, and his relationships with the other senior managers had continued to improve. Donato had been especially supportive.

But in spite of all the positive signs, the tension in the household had been steadily building right up to the morning of the long-awaited meeting. Jim had summed it all up when he left for work. "Well Karen," he said, "today is D day. I don't suppose it will take that long for me to know their decision. I'll call you as soon as I get out of the meeting with Philippe."

Karen stared once more at the telephone. It rang as if by command. She picked it up before the second ring.

"Hello, Karen."

"I've been waiting for your call. What happened?"

"Good news," was Jim's reply.

Karen felt like a huge bubble had burst in her rib cage as her tension dissipated. "Great! What did Philippe say?"

"He came right out and said that he and Katherine were very pleased that I had been able to turn the corner. In fact, Philippe said I had come around faster than they thought possible."

"That must have come as a huge relief."

"Sure did. Even though I thought things were going well, I felt this cloud of doubt hanging over me. I knew I wouldn't be able to really relax until I heard the words come out of their mouths," said Jim.

"What time did you go in to Philippe's office?"

"Right at eight-thirty."

"Eight-thirty?" Karen looked at her watch. "It's ten to ten."

"Philippe had a lot of other issues he wanted to discuss. He covered my situation in the first couple of minutes. Then he pulled out some files and started to discuss a number of HR issues with me."

"What kinds of things?" asked Karen.

"Fontaine was really interested in hearing about the performance spiral concept Peter taught me. We started talking about a companywide personal development program. We talked a lot about the personal management techniques I've been using. Apparently he got some very positive feedback from the employees who have been in the test program I've been running. Philippe asked me whether I thought all the employees could benefit from the techniques."

"What did you tell him?"

"I told him I thought that anyone could benefit from the concepts on a personal basis at the very least. And I said that there was a lot of potential to build better working relationships and performance at work. Then he started talking about Wilkinson."

"Oh?"

"Yeah. He started by making some general comments about Ted and the performance of the sales department. Then Philippe said that he realized that Wilkinson can be a pretty difficult guy to work with, and he complimented me for doing a better job coping with Ted lately," said Manion.

"How did you react to that?" asked Karen.

"I didn't reply right away. After I thought about it for a few seconds I told Fontaine that Ted could be difficult alright. But then I told him that we had to keep in mind that Wilkinson has some definite talents. You know, I've seen Ted deal with clients on some pretty touchy issues. The guy's pretty amazing. He always finds a way to establish some common ground with a customer," Manion answered.

"Given what you told me about how he treats the sales-people, I find it hard to believe that he can be accommodating with anyone," said Karen.

"I know Wilkinson really drives his people hard. Too hard. I already talked to Philippe about that a couple of months ago, so he knows my view about that."

"I can't feel the least bit positive about Ted," said Karen. "I guess I still remember that time you came home in a foul mood after having to deal with him. I can't forgive him for putting you through that."

"Some of it was my own fault for letting him get to me. Anyway, I've learned to brush off most of his comments. And I try to hide my reaction to the digs that do get through. I've turned it into a little game. Peter told me to observe him and learn to identify his patterns of behavior so I could deal with Ted more effectively. Once I got to understand Ted's behavior better, it became really tough watching a scenario play out between him and someone else. I could see ahead of time where the conversation was heading, but usually there wasn't much I could do to help the other person. The whole thing moves so quickly that it's hard to jump in to try to diffuse it. Once in a while I get lucky and I can jump in successfully. Usually witnessing him with other people helps me deal with him realistically when it's my turn."

"I don't want to talk about Wilkinson anymore," said Karen. "What else did you and Fontaine discuss?"

"Philippe wants me to help a number of the other departments implement some employee involvement programs. Apparently Fisher is really impressed with the improvements we've been able to make using employee input from the cross-functional product launch teams."

"That sounds like it could be a lot of fun."

"I'm really looking forward to it. The other thing Philippe wanted me to think about was working with him to design some simplified project management training. He was impressed with my participation on the employee involvement committee and found my project management approach very useful. He wants to implement a process that all of our employees could use. He felt it would really help people keep focused on their department objectives. I told him I'd be more than happy to lend a hand. He also wants to expand the personal management training. I suggested that we consider bringing Peter in for a train-the-trainer session," Manion explained.

"What was Philippe's reaction to that?" asked Karen.

"Positive. He said that his schedule is in pretty good shape toward the middle of next month, and he suggested I set up a meeting with Peter so all three of us can discuss the matter further," replied Manion.

Karen looked up as her secretary placed a note on her desk. "Jim, I have to run. I've got a major client holding on another line."

"Hang on a second. . . . "

"What?"

"I'm getting a sitter for the kids tonight. I want to take you out for dinner to celebrate. I couldn't have done it without you," said Jim.

A smile spread across Karen's face. "See you tonight."

24

As PHILIPPE FONTAINE APPROACHED KATHERINE FISHER'S office she motioned for him to join her at the conference table. Philippe entered, closed the door behind him, then sat in the chair next to Katherine.

"Thanks for following up on that sales department research for me, Philippe. What did you find out?"

"Just as I suspected. The first two regional sales managers I called completely supported Jacobsen. They confirmed that Ted has been verbally abusive with them for the past two years or so. So then I spoke with more of the field people, and I learned that there have also been instances in which Ted was totally out of line and threatened his people with transfers or dismissal. I looked up the people's files, and there didn't appear to be any cause for him to take that kind of action."

"You followed through and contacted all the field people?" asked Katherine.

"Yes. Just as you instructed. I made a number of discreet telephone calls. I told the field people that I was working on a survey to gauge employee satisfaction and the effectiveness of our senior management. I explained that I needed them to be absolutely candid with me so I could get a clear assessment of what issues should be addressed," replied Fontaine.

He opened a file folder so he could refer to his notes. "With most of them it didn't take long. After a couple of minutes they began to open up. I asked them what kinds of things bothered them the most. Some of the folks were careful with their choice of words, but they still managed to be very forthcoming about the treatment they had been subjected to. Others had no problem citing specific examples in which they thought management was out of line."

"Any comments about Wilkinson?"

"Plenty, . . . and none of them complimentary."

"Were you able to get anything really concrete?"

"I think a few of the guys must have been talking to Jacobsen, because they knew that the transfer Ted had been trying to force on him had been shelved. They didn't have any reservations about talking about specific threats Ted had made or some of the screaming sessions they'd endured with him. His people were always on the receiving end."

A deep furrow etched Katherine's brow. "How long has this been going on?"

"Katherine, we've always known Ted to be a pretty demanding boss, but he seems to have crossed the line from demanding to abusive about two years ago," Fontaine replied.

"So that puts it at about the time we made Donato a vice president and Manion was in the limelight with the new product launch," said Katherine.

"That's how it looks to me as well," Philippe replied.

"What's their view of the rest of the senior management team?" asked Katherine.

Philippe studied Fisher for a moment. "You really want to know?"

Katherine's eyes widened. "Of course I really want to know."

"By and large they think we're totally out of touch with reality. They can't believe the senior team didn't know about Wilkinson. So naturally they assumed we condoned his actions."

"How could they possibly think that?"

Philippe looked at Katherine. "Put yourself in their shoes. They've suffered with an abusive manager for years, and his behavior just keeps getting worse. No one in senior management pays any attention. No one asks them how they're doing. In short, no one seems to give a damn about them. What else are they supposed to think?"

Fontaine closed his file folder. "I was talking to Manion a couple of weeks ago, telling him we were happy with his turnaround. We got into a discussion about the personal management process he used to get himself squared around. During our discussions, Jim explained how our perceptions of other people are responsible for determining the nature of our relationships with them. I remembered that when I was talking to the field people. They probably see us as aloof, distant, uncaring."

Philippe paused noticeably. "And I'm not sure if I really know how we perceive them. I don't think our perceptions could be very positive. Otherwise wouldn't we have paid a lot more attention to what's been going on with them? I don't think it's fair for us to hold Wilkinson solely responsible for how he's treated his people. After all, we allowed it to happen."

"We don't encourage any of our management people to be abusive with their people. In fact, there are written policies that deal with that issue specifically. From what you've said, some of Ted's actions may be in clear violation of those policies. We could hang him out to dry," Katherine noted.

"Could we?" asked Fontaine. "Just because we have policies doesn't really mean anything if we haven't trained our managers to implement them. Policies don't mean much if we haven't enforced them when managers have crossed the line."

Policies don't mean much if they aren't enforced.

Katherine leaned back in her chair, away from the conference table. She sat in silence looking at Fontaine for several minutes. Finally she spoke. "You're right, Philippe. As much as I hate to admit it, we have neglected some of our management obligations, especially with the field people. Part of me would love to toss Ted's butt out of here tomorrow. But what he's done is only a symptom of a larger issue. We haven't developed our people management skills, our leadership skills. I have to take ultimate responsibility for that shortcoming. There's no excuse. We got out of touch with what was happening in the field. We blew it."

"We can take steps to correct those issues," said Fontaine. "In many respects that's the easy part. The difficulty is finding a way to deal with Wilkinson."

"What's your feeling?"

"As a management group we have to share the responsibility for his actions. We didn't exercise the foresight and follow-through we needed to live up to our personnel policies. We could cut him loose since some of his actions run contrary to company policy, or we could work with him to try to modify his behavior. He does have skills that are valuable to the company."

"Philippe, how are the field people going to react if Ted stays on? You've been talking to them. They're not stupid. They can read between the lines. Some of them must have put two and two together and figured out you were trying to get a handle on Wilkinson. I'm sure most of them have been exchanging notes since then. I'll bet a lot of them are hoping for a big change as far as Ted's concerned. What little morale is left out in the field could be destroyed if they don't see any positive changes in the management of the sales department."

"I think we can give the field guys more credit than that," Philippe responded. "They've been performing well under difficult circumstances for the past couple of years. From a practical perspective let's say we cut Ted loose. Then what? The board just approved our major plant expansion because we convinced them sales would show a strong rebound. We know Ted can get us the numbers in the short term. Bringing in someone new could stall the sales effort, especially since Ted already has close relationships with most of our major accounts. Do we want to take that risk going into the back end of the year when we really need the increase in sales and the board is looking over our shoulders?"

"We can't just let Ted keep doing what he's been doing!"

"Of course not. We need to address the issue very forcefully with him. The bottom line is that he's the best horse we have right now, and the race has already started."

"So we get through a few more months and then axe him? That doesn't make sense to me."

"Underneath the bravado, I think Wilkinson's a pragmatist. He knows he has a good position here, with excellent compensation. I don't think he'd throw that away on a whim. Maybe we can salvage him. A few months ago we had some serious doubts about Manion, too, and look how that's turned around. Maybe there's a way we can get Jim to work with Wilkinson?"

Katherine winced. "Do you think Wilkinson's ego could handle that? That sounds like we'd be lighting the wick on a stick of dynamite then asking Manion to hold it and wait for it to blow up."

"We'd obviously need to talk this over with Jim to see whether he'd agree to do it. The fact is Wilkinson has some talents the company can use. He also needs a lot of management development, and he has some performance and behavior problems he needs to tackle. I think Jim could really help him. Sure, Ted may simply put up with the coaching until he finds something else. But I think we have to make the effort to turn him around. He didn't get off track by himself."

Fisher looked at Fontaine pensively. "Let's suppose we do it. How do we monitor the progress and keep Wilkinson in line?"

"I think the key is to get Ted's current performance, and the company's expectations for change, documented. Remembering how we handled Jim, I think we need to approach Wilkinson a bit differently because Wilkinson definitely contravened company policy on a number of occasions. We should document all the issues thoroughly," said Fontaine.

Fisher nodded.

Fontaine continued, "Obviously we have to bring Manion into the loop early on to see if he'd be willing to coach Ted. If he is, we'll need to give him a lot of rein on how to handle the issue with Wilkinson. From a control and monitoring perspective, we could have Jim supply me with a weekly status report, of which Ted would be fully aware. I could do some selected interviews with the field staff every month to gauge progress."

"OK. That might work."

"I think we should throw the ball to Manion and let him decide if and how he might want to be involved with getting Wilkinson turned around. I think Jim will do it, and there are two probable outcomes: either he'll be successful and get Wilkinson turned around, or Ted will ignore the help but clean up his act in the short term until he finds something else. Either way I think we will be taking some stress off the field force and maintaining our momentum with our sales efforts at this critical time of year. If a month or so goes by and Ted isn't making any real progress we can start a quiet search for a replacement. The bottom line is companies hire people based on skills and fire them because of attitudes.

Companies hire people based on skills and fire them because of attitudes.

Regardless of what happens with Ted, we need to reassess our priorities as a management team. We need to focus on the people issues a lot more."

Philippe's head bowed slightly. "Damn it! I missed the boat on this one. I should have been aware of Wilkinson's actions." He looked up at Katherine. "We owe it to our people never to let this happen again."

25

Manion arrived at the office at seven. He completed some work on a couple of urgent files then organized the other projects he had for the day. At nine-fifteen he put his telephone on call forward and closed the door to his office.

After getting comfortable in his chair, Jim began to practice his relaxation exercise. Within a few minutes he felt the familiar easing of tension. On this particular day he definitely wanted to stay composed.

Manion took out his affirmation cards and sorted through them, picking two he specifically wanted to reinforce. He began to practice his visualizations. Satisfied that he was sufficiently focused, Jim then began to rehearse for his upcoming meeting with Ted Wilkinson.

He knew that within the next fifteen minutes Wilkinson would be coming out of his meeting with Katherine Fisher and Philippe Fontaine. Ted would have the results of Philippe's follow-up interviews with the regional sales managers. He'd also know that he was being put on notice for his abusive behavior. Jim ran numerous scenes through his mind trying to anticipate all of the various possible reactions he might expect from Wilkinson. Manion knew this initial meeting would be critical if there was any hope of helping Ted salvage his position with the company.

Jim glanced at his watch. It was almost nine-thirty. Manion reached over to his telephone and took it off call forward. He waited for it to ring.

His patience was rewarded in a couple of minutes.

"Good morning, Jim Manion speaking."

"Jim, Philippe. We've just finished our meeting with Wilkinson. He wanted to return a couple of customer calls before he started his meeting with you. He should be over in about five minutes."

"How did it go?" Manion asked.

"Icy cold. It was hard to get a reading on how he took the news."

"Do you think he was surprised at all?"

"Somewhat," replied Fontaine. "Although my guess is that he already had some indications from a couple of regional sales managers that I had been talking to the field people."

"Any words of wisdom?"

"Not really. You have a copy of the letter Wilkinson received this morning, so you know exactly what we expect from him and the timetable attached to it. By the way, thanks for taking such an active interest in helping to develop the plan. Without your input I doubt we would have been willing to give him six months to get his behavior on track."

"Well Philippe, I think looking at the recovery as a three-stage process is a lot more realistic. That way we can give him some feedback on his progress every couple of months. If he starts to get off track, we'll have a better chance of catching it and working with him," said Manion.

"Good luck this morning, Jim."

Manion hung up the telephone and continued to run

some images of the pending meeting through his mind. A few minutes later there was a tap on his door.

"I'm supposed to see you this morning," Wilkinson said as he entered the room.

"Good morning, Ted, come on in. Let's sit at the conference table," Jim replied as he put his telephone on call forward.

Wilkinson sat down and stared coldly at Manion.

Manion joined him at the table. "Look Ted, let's not beat around the bush. I know this isn't going to be easy for you. I've been involved in some of the meetings with Fisher and Fontaine, so I'm aware of the substance of your discussions with them this morning."

"I thought you would be."

Jim noticed Wilkinson's right heel tapping nervously on the carpet. "Ted, the ball is in your court. It's up to you to decide if you still want to be in the game. All I can tell you is that I'm prepared to give you whatever help I can to see you through this."

The muscles around Ted's jaw twitched. "You'll understand if I'm more than a little skeptical."

Manion collected his thoughts. "Yeah, I guess I understand how you might feel. It really boils down to whether you want to trust me. All I can ask you to do is to think back a few months. I could have made things pretty ugly for you at that board meeting, but I chose not to."

Jim waited for a reply from Wilkinson. None came. Manion walked over to his desk and picked up the bolt Miller had given him. "A friend of mine gave me this bolt as a gift four months ago. He used it to explain the continuous performance spiral we're all on."

Ted lifted his head and glanced at the bolt.

Jim spun the nut a few revolutions. "None of us is static, Ted. We're either improving our performance like this, or declining like this. We all get on a downward spiral from time to time."

Manion looked intently at the bolt as he continued speaking. "I've had my share of difficult times like everyone else."

He raised his eyes and made contact with Wilkinson. "Everything starts with how we perceive the world around us, Ted. You can choose to view me as an ally. If you do, we'll develop a much better relationship than we've had in the past. An improved relationship will create a lot of potential between us. We'll have an opportunity to work on some specific activities that will help you get beyond the current situation. I'm willing to try. But that's not enough."

Wilkinson looked steely-eyed at Manion. "It's not like we've been best buddies."

"No, we haven't. And on a personal basis we don't have to be," answered Manion.

He got a pad of paper and a pen from his desk. "Ted, let's look at this as a project." Jim drew two circles on either side of the page. "You're here. Fisher and Fontaine have given you a target to reach over here in six months." Manion drew a line to connect the two circles. "It's going to take some time and effort for you to make the change. If you keep doing what you've been doing, you won't have any chance of getting there. I want to help you manage that change, Ted. I can share some techniques that helped me out of a difficult situation. It's your choice."

Manion put the bolt on the conference table.

Wilkinson reached over and picked it up. He spun the nut up and down the shaft of the bolt several times. "I'll have to think about this for a few days." Ted looked at Manion as he placed the bolt back down on the table. "Is there anything else?"

"Not unless there's something else you want to talk about," Manion replied.

Wilkinson shook his head. "No, I think I've had about all I can handle today."

After Ted left the office Manion picked up the bolt and went back to his desk, reached for the telephone, and called Philippe. "Just finished my meeting with Wilkinson. I think it went about as well as could be expected. It's been a rough day for him."

"Did you get a reaction?"

"Not much. He was pretty cool. It might not have been a total waste, though. He said he'd consider looking at the performance enhancement techniques we talked about."

"Well, we'll see what happens," Fontaine replied. "Keep me posted."

Manion hung up the telephone. He reflected on the four months since Peter Miller had given him the bolt. A smile crept over his face. He picked up the telephone and dialed Peter's number.

"Morning, Peter. It's Jim. I just got through with my meeting with Wilkinson."

"Did it go as expected?" asked Peter.

"Uh-huh. You were right, Peter. Wilkinson was very cool and aloof through the whole thing. I practiced a number of mental rehearsals where I pictured Ted having more emotional reactions, but I didn't need them," replied Manion.

"We're dealing with a pretty controlled character, especially at this point. I didn't think he'd do anything rash," Miller said.

"What do you think he'll do next?"

"I think he'll make a few calls later today or tomorrow. I'm dead positive the first call will be to his lawyer to check on the actions of the company. You can bet if all the *i*'s haven't been dotted and the *t*'s haven't been crossed properly, he'll come back in attack mode. Assuming that the company has everything locked up and airtight, my best guess is that he'll sit in the weeds waiting for you folks to make a mistake. . . . Then he'll attack. You'd better stay in close contact with Fontaine and make sure everyone follows the script perfectly," Peter advised.

Manion's lips drew tight. He nodded his head in silent agreement. "I knew it seemed too easy today."

"This is only round one," said Miller. "He's not going to just lie down for you."

"But what choice does he have, really?" asked Manion. "He's got his formal letter from the company. He's been put on notice."

"True enough, but if Ted's lawyer thinks you haven't handled everything perfectly he might advise Ted to launch a suit against the company."

"Are you saying there's no hope of turning him around?"

"Of course there's hope. I was just describing his initial reactions to the situation. The biggest stumbling block right now is in Wilkinson's own head. If he can accept that you genuinely want to help him, he may open up enough for you to start the process with him. Remember, you can't change him. You can only help people who are willing to help themselves."

Manion's gaze settled on the stainless-steel bolt Miller had given him. Extending his right arm and picking it up, Jim studied the bolt for a moment and smiled. He rotated the nut counterclockwise so it climbed up the stem.

"Peter, how can I ever repay you for all you've done for me? I don't know how I could have straightened things out without you. You've helped me understand how to get in touch with my perceptions and live on the upside of the performance spiral. . . . You've helped me see the use of project management in my personal life, given me all the personal performance techniques. You've done so much."

"Just make me one promise," said Miller.

"Name it."

Miller let out a hearty laugh. "Promise that you'll invest twenty minutes in yourself every day. I don't know if I could survive turning you around another time!"

Invest twenty minutes in yourself every day. You're worth it.

Index

About the Author

Thomas Stirr has worked as a manager in sales, marketing, and advertising for the past twenty years with a number of major North American corporations. His work has been acknowledged by fifteen industry recognition awards. These include two Sheppard Awards of Merit that honor outstanding business-to-business advertising, a Silver Award in the Canadian Direct Marketing Association's prestigious RSVP competition, and three Best Display trade show awards. He has been a regular columnist with *Marketing* magazine and has participated in industry events as a guest speaker and panelist.

Thomas Stirr speaks to organizations and community groups on a range of personal performance issues. Some of these topics include: the impact of self-image and attitude on performance communications, the importance of building self-esteem, and the effective use of project management at work and as a life skill.

WE WOULD LOVE TO HEAR FROM YOU

We hope that **Miller's Bolt: A Modern Business Parable** has given you many practical techniques you can use to improve your personal performance, build more productive relationships, and better manage the stresses and changes in your life.

If you would like to make any comments about **Miller's Bolt: A Modern Business Parable**, or contact Thomas Stirr, please write:

> Thomas-Ritt Associates
> 1 Main St. W., Box 20032
> Grimsby, On L3M 5J3
> CANADA